Married to COACH SUBMITTED TO BOTH

SHARING OUR LIVES WITH COACH AND CHRIST
A 31 DAY PRAYER DEVOTIONAL FOR COACHES' WIVES

CECELIA **SIMON**

For permission please submit email to: caterpillarstransformed@gmail.com

Unless otherwise indicated, Scripture quotations are from the ESV Bible. The ESV® Bible (The Holy Bible, English Standard Version®). ESV® Text Edition: 2016. Copyright © 2001 by Crossway, a publishing ministry of Good News Publishers. The ESV® text has been reproduced in cooperation with and by permission of Good News Publishers. Used by permission. All rights reserved.

Scripture quotations marked NIV are from the Holy Bible, New Living Translation, copyright © 1996, 2004, 2015 by Tyndale House Foundation. Used by permission of Tyndale House Publishers, Inc., Carol Stream, Illinois 60188. All rights reserved.

Scripture references marked MSG are taken from The Holy Bible, The Message is quoted: "Scripture taken from The Message. Copyright © 1993, 1994, 1995, 1996, 2000, 2001, 2002. Used by permission of NavPress Publishing Group.

Scripture references marked NIV are taken from The Holy Bible, New International Version®, NIV® Copyright © 1973, 1978, 1984, 2011 by Biblica, Inc.® Used by permission. All rights reserved worldwide.

All emphasis in Scripture have been added by the author.

ISBN 978-0-692-12541-0

Cover design: Demarcus McGaughey
Author photo: Daniel Kwon
Formatting: Shannon Herring - ChristianEditingServices.com

To coaches' wives, who understand this life the best,
ya'll give me courage.

Joshua 1:9

To my husband, John,
thank you for giving me your last name.

Mark 10:8

Contents

It's Halftime!

Third Quarter: When Passion Meets Purpose

Fourth Quarter: Bowl or Bust?

Introduction

et's just start off with some honesty here. Fall has never been my favorite season. I prefer spring or summer. I'm a Southern Girl. Blame it on my southern roots. The chilling temperatures leading up to the winter months of frost, freezing rain, and potential snow don't tickle my fancy. I'm well aware, too, that it's the time of year when I see my husband the least and time of year when I will have to take our two sons to football practices, games and after school extra-curricular activities alone. On top of that, I have to accept that this is the time of the year when I have the responsibility of dealing with some of the rudest fans in the stands, spitting off at the mouth about what they would do if they were the coach and how they would do it. Oh yes, honey! This is Football season , and it comes around every year like clockwork!

Now, don't get me wrong. From a positive perspective, the chill in the air, the smell of hot chocolate, cheesy nachos, grilled burgers, and popcorn in the concession stands definitely heighten my anticipation. Oh, the buttery smell of popcorn…give me two tubs full, please!

Then there are the fans who guzzle gallons of beer, I meant soda (this is a Christian book), during halftime, and that has its highs and lows after the tipsy sets in. Lest we forget, the stare from the rivals team that, like a laser beam, pierces through one's soul. The finalizing of tailgating plans, the perfect game day outfit, and the road trips to cheer on your favorite team. These are, just to name a few, coaches' wives' highlights. YES, football is all about fun, being with family, friends, and fans, but what I've learned over time is that you can't have football without having a little FAITH. It's all obsolete if God isn't in it.

Just like quarters, players, and positions change in the game of football, the season of Fall brings about positive change, as well. It is the season when the trees and their bright iridescence illuminate our highways and neighborhoods. If we're lucky, those beautiful yellow, red, and orange leaves liven' up our yards and give our children hours of play as they jump from pile to pile of gorgeously attractive colors. It is the season when we give thanks and gather in family and friends' kitchens smelling the aroma of Mom's favorite cornbread dressing or Grandmother's incomparable cream cheese pound cake, if we're lucky to get away from a Thanksgiving kickoff. Fall leads up to the time of the year when we celebrate the birth of our Lord and Savior Jesus Christ, we enjoy the season of giving, and we reflect on all the blessings the previous and present year has bestowed upon us.

The breathtaking aroma of apple cider and pumpkin spice are familiar smells that remind me every year of football season, and there's absolutely no way around it. As a result, I've learned to love what my husband loves, care about what he cares about, and I've learned, just as he did in his small beginnings at five years old, to give my all to what **we've** put so much time and passion into. It has become a part of who we are as #TEAMSIMON , and it is what we will forever be *growing* into as long as we are in this profession.

Football has given us so much more than we've ever bargained for in life and love. We've had our share of ups and downs, as I'm certain many of you have too, but the good has always outweighed the bad. The fall season reminds us after "falling" to get back up and be thankful whenever life tries to knock us down. It has been a constant reminder to give thanks IN ALL THINGS. The fall is a reminder, for John and I, that just as the beautiful colors of the leaves change, so will our situation. The crisp chill brings the beauty of the fallen leaves and the fullness of restoration when we walk out this season in our lives with faith. For us, hope in this season comes from choosing a positive perspective about everything that may come our way. Though things may happen to us, we won't allow them to get *in* us because for us, the difference from August to December is knowing what to bite off and chew and what to leave at the concession stand.

Over time, these 19 years of dating, courting, and married life with football has taught me many lessons that I'd like to share with my fellow coaches' wives in this devotional. Herein lies the bible verses I've had to lean on in seasons of drought and the prayers I've prayed when my hope was diminishing, when I cried myself to sleep because my husband was on the road recruiting and I was home alone with our two boys, when I went to awards ceremonies, parent/teacher conferences, and school assemblies without him because duty called, when I graduated from God's Leading Ladies Life Enrichment Program from the Potter's House Church in Dallas, Texas and my favorite coach wasn't there in the audience to clap for me because those Friday night lights didn't go out to acknowledge my accomplishment… there were no timeouts scheduled for him to watch me walk across the stage or sit with me at the doctor's office for our 6th grader's 11 year old wellness check-up vaccinations.

The great thing about football, however, is that you can be down on the score board, make turnovers, and lose yardage in the first half of the game, but if you hold on to your faith, there is a second half after you rest, regroup, and refocus to allow for a turn around. The key is to not get caught up in the scoreboard and lose focus in the beginning. The win is always earned by the one who fights 'til the end! Life is similar in so many ways.

From Little League to the National Football League, my coach and I have seen it all. My resolve, through it all, has been Jesus. He has ALWAYS been there to lead and guide every one of our footsteps. When I couldn't trace His hands, I believed his heart was for me and my family. When I was unsure of our next move, what school our boys would attend, where the safest neighborhoods were located…I depended on the Holy Spirit to guide us. When I questioned if our boys would adapt to their new environment and find new friends I believed that all things would work together for our good. When I wondered if my husband's team would ever win a game, or if I would be accompanied by his presence at the next baseball tournament, I learned to trust God. PERIOD. And for that, I am grateful.

Go with me through the season of football, family, and faith, if you would. I guess you don't have an option now. You bought the devotional and you've read up to this point, so you might as well keep going. I pray it blesses you on your journey as a coach's wife, be it football, basketball, or baseball…soccer, cheerleading, or swimming. My prayer is that you find Him in your uncertainty just as my family has. Jesus is our stability, and the only thing we've found to be consistent on this football journey we've traveled thus far.

Father,

Thank you for this devotional you have given me to share with other coaches' wives. I pray you speak into their lives and into their circumstances, specifically. It is my prayer they find you here and you meet every one of their needs according to your will for their lives.

May each and every coach's wife reading this devotional individually, in a group, or in their team's coaches' wives' circle, for the next 31 days, find their hope, their confidence, and their trust in You and You alone.

In your name I ask it, seek it, and believe it is already so.

In Jesus' name, Amen!

Before we begin the first quarter, let's introduce some home field advantage rules. It is my hope that this becomes more than a book for you to open up and read over the next 31 days in your leisure. I really do pray that you settle your mind from all outside and inside distractions and find quiet time to comprehend what is being written in this book.

In these moments for the next 31 days, I implore you to take notes, write down a plan of action and answer questions about yourself, that warrant real answers, that you may have never answered before. Why? Because truth is reality, and if we don't recognize and embrace our truth, then we really don't know who we are. And if we don't know who we are, we can't change or help anyone else. Knowing our truth, that is written in the Scriptures, in God's Word is the first step to a transformed life.

To help with your time of reflection, there will be a little bit of homework for you to do after each devotional, a moment each day that should provoke an action from you that comes from within. Why? Simply because God wants you to grow spiritually, and ultimately He desires for you to become His friend. To know Him, you must do more than just ask Him to be your savior through salvation. The hard work actually begins AFTER you become His child. The next responsibilities in becoming a part of Christ's family is studying and learning His ways, applying His principles, and being transformed by what is written in His Word for the rest of your life. This, my friends, is the daily process of Christian living. It's what sets you apart from the rest. A life of devotion will last longer than 31 days. It will take dedication and practice for the rest of your life. Just like becoming a better coach and football player, you won't become a pro-Christian overnight

(I don't think any of us ever will), but the goal in studying God's Word is to better understand what Jesus said and did so that we become more faithful to the calling He has placed on our individual lives and in our marriages.

If you don't understand a Bible verse that I have included in this devotional, read the passage that the verse came from. If the passage is unclear, and you still don't understand the verse, read the chapter in the Bible where the passage came from. And if after reading the chapter you're still not sure, read the entire book. For example: the book of Matthew or the book of Ruth. Oh, and be sure to get yourself a good study bible also, one with footnotes and references. I like to use the English Standard Version Student Study Bible or the New Living Translation. These make the reading and understanding a lot more engaging and comprehendible for me, but I am certainly not suggesting that you limit your studies to these. It is totally up to you to use what you have on hand or to find a Bible that you prefer to use.

As for the homework after each day's devotional, there are three parts to help you gather your thoughts and apply the reading to your life:

1. illumination
2. application
3. transformation

Reading with focus on illumination, application, and transformation will stretch you to **think** a certain way, **believe a certain way** (the Bible's spiritual truth), and **do** things a certain way (what the Bible tells you to do for your life and for your marriage). Each topic's very basic meaning is explained in extension below:

1.) Illumination

This is when the bible narrative becomes meaningful to your life. A lightbulb comes on. The Holy Spirit causes you to think of ways you currently operate. You get to see with clarity if your actions please God or are displeasing to Him. Moving forward, you get to assess your life, through Scripture, to see what's needed to look like the image Jesus has called you to emulate.

2.) Application

This is when you move from thinking to doing. It is when you move from reading mere wording in the bible to a conscious awareness of studying and obedience to do what it says. According to Henrichson and Jackson, in their writings *Studying, Interpreting, and Applying the Bible*, "application must be focused on pleasing God rather than pleasing others."

It's the *DO* part.

3.) Transformation

This is when the image of what we desire to look like becomes less important than the holy image God requires for us to seek after in Genesis 1:27. This should be the goal of all mankind, especially Christians.

After the Holy Spirit has stretched your thinking through illumination and you are no longer ignorant to the truth, then application of the truth in God's Word is your next step. You must do what it says. This is the responsibility of all Believers for the rest of their lives. Lastly, transformation takes place when you do not conform to what the world and everything that is around you is doing. Instead, you are strategic in finding the righteous behaviors of Christ, specifically by the instructions in Romans 12:2.

Let's get started, shall we?

First Quarter:

One Band, One Sound

When John and I discussed writing a devotional on our experiences in coaching, I never thought that it to be so beneficial for me. When we sat down to organize and outline this devotional, I wasn't quite sure what that would look like, but was grateful in the end that it happened the way it did.

When we decided to write this book together a couple of summers ago, we took out paper and pencil and put our thoughts on paper right there at the kitchen table. What I didn't realize was that my coach was actually about to sit down and share his heart with me, and that the information I would write would be so much more than black and white.

He discussed his feelings and heartfelt prayers about every aspect of his coaching career. He shared things like what to expect and what to pray for as his wife. He talked about what other coaches had experienced and felt and offered ways to pray for their situations too. John wrote down what he thought we as coaches' wives should know in each quarter of football and most importantly, what prayers we should be covering our husbands, brothers, uncles, and friends with at those particular times.

My first thoughts were, *"WOW, Dude! I didn't know all of that was going on. I didn't know you felt that way. Most importantly, I didn't know I should have been praying about those particular things in those situations."* Perhaps, if we would have never sat down to write this together, I would've never known any of the information he shared. The mere fact that he was transparent, open, and vulnerable was a blessing in writing this devotional for all of you and for me. I hope, that maybe... just maybe this coaches' wives devotional will open up dialogue between you and your coach to discuss his fears, his frustrations, and his faith in God.

I pray it blesses you as much as it blessed me to sit down and hear, first hand, from the heart of my FAVORITE Coach about what this life is like on and off the field. I believe our hearts beat the same rhythm now. Our harmony resonates to the heavens. God is pleased with the tune of unison. We are one in marriage, faith, family, and football.

> *"How good and pleasant it is when God's people live together in unity... for there the Lord commanded the blessing - life forevermore!"*
> *Psalm 133:1,3*

1

Purpose Positioning

"For I have come down from heaven, not to do my own will but the will of him who sent me."
John 6:38

After living in Dallas, TX for eight years, to say the least, we were comfortable. It was the longest place we'd lived the longest in John's professional football career, and I was content—content with our normal, content with our church, and grateful that we hadn't loaded any boxes and/or a U-Haul since my husband's National Football League career had ended. Both of our sons were born in Texas, they started school there, and John and I had started over from the life that we knew to embrace the reality of what had totally slapped us in the face. After a shoulder injury, John's career in the NFL was over. Life for us began all over again.

I was pregnant with our first son during our move to Dallas. Both were a surprise—the baby and the boxes. Nevertheless, life was happening. It wasn't speeding up, but it most certainly wasn't slowing down. John and I began our little family during this time and then decided to go back to school and get our Master's degrees. Both of us. At the same time. To the same school. And did I mention I was pregnant now with our second son?

After three years total, our Master's degrees were completed. We did it together. What an accomplishment! We were established, we were acclimated, and we were being still…in one place… finally! Life was moving for us in a good way, as long as there were no trucks involved and things were finally starting to stabilize. By then, I was serving in our church and had even started my own mentorship program at the middle school where I taught 6th grade. In the words of my dear friend and coach's wife, Lisa, "Life was good! All good!" The boys were growing, John was the head coach and athletic director of a high school and Team Simon was being fruitful.

Then, one day out of the blue, my husband came home from work and shared his aspiration with me to one day become a college coach. Yeah, the guy who was injured in practice. The guy who said he wasn't going to coach or touch another football in his life after his sudden release from the League. Yeah, that guy with the bitter football taste in his mouth wanted to do what?

Each day, as time passed, the itch to fulfill his goal grew larger and became more and more intense until it was unbearable to soothe. He'd done most of his part to climb the ladder, yet he lacked graduate assistance coaching experience on the collegiate level. It's what we thought he needed for him to obtain this position. But God's thoughts were different.

God arrested my thoughts and physical disposition one day in my 6th grade classroom about five minutes before the bell was about to ring for me to receive my next group of students. As I sat at my desk enjoying quiet moments during my lunch break, scarfing down the last few crumbs of my turkey sandwich, God gave me this message for my husband. It was so profound that I wrote it down and took a picture and have kept it stored and tucked away for all these years! His sweet presence that day in that classroom in Dallas, TX had me in tears!

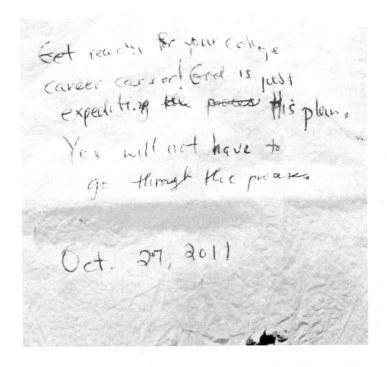

It reads, *"Get ready for your college career. God is just expediting His plan. You will not have to go through the process. October 27, 2011."*

Y'all, this is a picture of the original napkin that I still have stashed away in the binder from the God's Leading Ladies Program I graduated from that my husband wasn't able to attend. I have taken it along this coaching journey with us to remind us that everywhere we go, God's faithfulness, favor, and grace is with us.

As you can see, according to the scribbles, I couldn't write fast enough. The pen just wasn't cooperating. The presence of God engulfed my classroom that day like bees swarm a honey comb. His presence was just that sweet and evident! I could barely gather myself for the next class that was knocking at my door as I wiped tears of worship from my face, not exactly understanding what it all meant, but trusting God would reveal himself in due season.

A year and a half later in December 2012, God didn't renege on his promise, but showed himself mighty! John got the call to join the University of Southern Mississippi as their running backs coach with no prior graduate assistance experience. God, indeed, expedited my husband's career and he didn't have to go through the process just as the napkin said. As for the phone call, it couldn't have come at a better time. We were headed to Las Vegas to celebrate John's 34th birthday. To the birthday celebration toast, we added his new career!

As pointed out, I was writing so fast, I wrote the word "career" twice. Then I had to scratch out words to make sure I only wrote what God was telling me to tell my husband. The same goes for life. Some things will happen so quickly that you won't have time to comprehend them, but move anyway! Before you know it, someone will knock on the door and you will be thrown into your next assignment. This is why it's important to, make sure you are in tune with the Word of God and you're available when He's ready to invade your space and instruct you on your next move. New seasons, most times, bring about a sudden change. Therefore, you must not allow distractions to get in your way. God will give you the power to keep going, but you've got to hear from Him and know exactly what He is instructing you to do, not just for you, but for others.

I often wonder why God arrested me that day and not my husband. Who knows? Perhaps, he was too busy. Perhaps, he was distracted by work and other things. Maybe his mind wasn't clear because of all of his responsibilities. Nevertheless, I picked up the slack. I'm glad I was in position to hear. I'm grateful I was available and God used me as His messenger that day to run home, sobbing passionately, to show my husband the napkin and explain to him what took place in that 6th grade classroom in South Dallas.

There is a position God is calling you to, but your heart has to be right and your motives pure. It is a position that has been specifically designed with you in mind and no one else will be able to take it. Jesus created it just for you. But the position has nothing to do with you. It has everything to do with the glory of the Father. The prerequisite: lose your will, your plans, and your goals, for His. That is all.

d Christ

30 40 40 50 50 40 40 30 30 20 20 10

Purpose Positioning

Prayer

*God, thank you for purpose, for only what
we do for you will last in this life.
In Jesus' mighty name,
Amen!*

Application & Transformation

Illumination: What are your thoughts concerning this devotional? What is God asking you to believe?

_____
_____
_____
_____
_____

Application: What is God asking you to **DO**?

_____
_____
_____
_____
_____

Transformation: The Holy Spirit has revealed His character to you through this study. **_What is one thing you could change today that will make your character look more like His?_**

_____
_____
_____
_____
_____
_____

2

Purposeful Prayer

"Then you will call on me and come and pray to me,
and I will listen to you. You will seek me and find me when you
seek me with all your heart. I will be found by you, declares the Lord..."
Jeremiah 29:12-14

I find so much comfort in knowing that when we pray, God hears us, and not only does He hear us, but He listens. He has everything we need and knows our end from the beginning. As busy as He may seem, and as many issues as He may be faced with day to day, not just from us, but from other families, coaches' wives, and our country, His promises stand true.

Yes, we play a role in this dear journey we call life. One of those roles being that we establish a prayer life with God in the midst of our "To Do" lists. Yeah, I get it… the husband goes off to work and we're left with responsibilities that may not always get done in 24 hours. But those things are never more important than carving out time with God. He is the only one who will establish and sustain us. He is the one who gave your husband his job and has allowed that particular organization to provide for you in this season of your lives. Don't you dare desire God's presents more than His presence. After all, He wants to tell you something. He has some secrets to whisper in your ear. He wants to know that He's more important than your "To Do" list. He has some things to say to you about your husband.

Just as He arrested me that day in my classroom, He wants to arrest you too—for you, perhaps, or maybe like in my situation, for your husband or someone else in your family that is in need of a word from God. Jesus desires your whole heart because He has something to say that is vital to your life and He promises that when you give your whole heart to Him, it will not be in vain. He will show up in your situations and your circumstances, on your husband's job, and in your home. He will come see about you and turn your dark nights into dancing days. He wants to meet you at your point of need and invade your work space.

So, raise those children like a boss if that's your current position. Clean that house like nobody's business, and cook that dinner like your husband has never tasted it in his life. Change those diapers like a pro and sit in that car line at your kids' school with patience, knowing that this is not the end, but just the beginning. However, don't do all those things and forget to incorporate prayer into your busy day. You have a role to play and it may seem insignificant to you, but it's not insignificant to God. When you make time for a quiet moment, take notes, ask questions, be present, and pray. Carve out a little time for God each day, preferably before the alarm clocks go off, the baby wakes up for milk and the never ending requests and demands begin. Jesus will instruct you; He even wants to. You will find that being in His presence is never time wasted and it will become the very best moments of your day.

Purposeful Prayer

Prayer

Dear God,

Don't let us believe the lie that our days will be productive without you. Help us to remember that life will forever be empty if we leave you out of it. Thank you in advance for coming to see about us when we make you first in our lives. You've promised you will always be there. We are never alone, even though at times it may feel like it. We can trust you are only a prayer away. Remind us that our next move, next decision, and next big break is counting on us spending time in prayer and in your presence.

In the name of Jesus,
Amen!

Application & Transformation

Illumination: What are your thoughts concerning this devotional? What is God asking you to believe?

_____

_____

_____

_____

_____

Application: What is God asking you to **DO**?

_____

_____

_____

_____

Transformation: The Holy Spirit has revealed His character to you through this study. **_What is one thing you could change today that will make your character look more like His?_**

_____

_____

_____

_____

_____

3

On Assignment

*"So Jesus said to them. Truly, truly I say to you, the Son
can do nothing of his own accord, but only what he sees
the Father doing. For whatever the Father does,
that the Son does likewise."*
John 5:19

Contrary to popular belief, you and your husband's current position is not all about who's writing your paycheck. Not at all, my friend. It is so much more than X's and O's. The both of you have purpose to fulfill where you are, and passing the test in your current role is vital to where God desires to take you.

During our first year with John as a college coach, our team wasn't that good. In fact, the head coach and coaching staff took over a team that hadn't won any games the previous season. Things weren't looking so good from the beginning for us. It was a long, tough road, to wanting so very badly to win, yet, knowing the reality was that the program needed to be rebuilt and wasn't going to be rebuilt over night, or in the first year.

The week of our final game of the season had arrived and as I had been in prayer the entire season for the players, staff, university, community—everybody and anybody—I remember God giving me strategic and specific instructions during this prayer time. It was different from any other of our quiet moments that season because this time He wasn't so quiet.

Although I didn't write down this time what He told me to do, I remembered and I acted. I'm not crazy, so don't judge. I'm just radical for Christ! So, I courageously set out to do just what He said.

Jesus instructed me to take our boys, John and James, and go to the football facility. I thought, *"Okay, sure, I've been there before many times, I can do that,"* but there was a specific detail attached: Don't go without any anointing oil (olive oil that has been blessed by a minister or pastor). I thought, *"Okay...check. Got it."* So, I did exactly what Jesus said. This was on a Thursday evening. I packed my bottle of oil in my purse and the boys and I were well on our way up the highway headed to the football facility.

Here was another moment on this journey I didn't fully understand, but I was sure if He said it, He wouldn't lead me astray. I settled in my mind before the boys and I left the house that I was going to trust God.

I assured the boys along the way that we were going to visit Dad's office like we'd done many times before, and of course, they were all in! When we pulled up to the front door, the team was on the practice field as were all the coaches and other staff. GREAT! Access CONFIRMED!

I started up the stairs and into the building, oil in purse, boys by my side. I said to myself, "*What are we doing now, God?*" The Holy Spirit told me to go and pray over the football staff's offices. I thought, "*Piece of cake, that's easy,*" until I remembered I had our boys, John and James, with me, and they for sure wouldn't be as quiet as I would want them to be.

Unbeknownst to me, as I stepped off of the elevator onto the second floor where the football offices were located, in the sitting area was a brand spankin' new, 60 inch flat screen TV mounted on the wall! And lo and behold, the gigantic screen in front of us immediately grabbed both boys' attention as if we'd walked into the movie theater. And of course, what was playing on it? Highlights of the university's football games. Our boys, at the very young ages of five and seven, were mesmerized!

I asked the receptionist at the front desk if the boys could sit in the foyer next to the screen and wait for me and he said, "Yes, and I will watch them for you." Wait? What? WHEW! Nobody but God could set something up like that. Anywho...I felt like I had jumped over a hurdle and cleared it! "*See you guys in a second,*" I stated, and walked through the back to the coaches' offices.

Next, I took the oil out of my purse and rubbed it into both of my hands. As I made my rounds through the halls, I intentionally touched every Coach's door knob, praying for each one of them, individually, praying what the Holy Spirit was telling me to pray. When I got to my husband's office, I didn't touch just his door knob, but I went in and touched everything I could see—his desk, his chair, his computer, play book, name plate by his door—I touched everything in sight with the oil on my hands and prayed over it.

As I started for the door, I had left an office out. The head coach's office. It was on the same hall as my husband's. I could see it up the hallway as I exited John's door. When I got to the HC's door and stayed there a little bit longer, the prayer was different from the rest of the coaches.' God had revealed some things beyond football, and I continued to pray. Needless to say, I held on to his doorknob, and I wouldn't let go until God was done.

By that time, the coach over operations was rounding the corner, but the deed was done. I had already put my oil back in my purse, and I was headed to get the boys. I told the front desk receptionist thanks for watching them and as we we left, I took a deep sigh of relief going down on the elevator.

Needless to say, that Saturday, we WON our first game, which happened to be the last game of the season. Indeed, when I moved my thoughts, my feelings, and my emotions out of the way to hear God in prayer, I realized I was on assignment. It was well worth the risk to see the smiles on the players' faces upon their arrival home. The entire community welcomed them back to the facility, that God had me pray over two days prior, with signs, posters, big hugs, and cheers, congratulating them on their first victory all year. There was still hope for this football program after all, and I was just a small part of it.

I'll never forget overhearing my husband one day, telling his running backs, "You have one job when you get your opportunity out there on the field. Make sure you **know your assignment.**" The same is true for us. Do what God tells you to do, ladies, and if you don't know what that is, then just simply do what He does.

On Assignment

Prayer

God,

Help us to remember that our assignment is bigger than our feelings, emotions, and our logic. May we walk by faith, reassured in your promises, even when things don't make sense. May purpose ring louder than the distractions, and in prayer may we find our courage and strength. Help us to be brave even if that means standing and/or sneaking through hallways alone. Thank you in advance for giving us this assignment. You could have given it to anyone else, but you have trusted us to do it. Thank you for deeming us worthy.

In Jesus' name,
Amen!

Application & Transformation

Illumination: What are your thoughts concerning this devotional? What is God asking you to believe?

_____

_____

_____

_____

_____

Application: What is God asking you to **DO**?

_____

_____

_____

_____

Transformation: The Holy Spirit has revealed His character to you through this study. ***What is one thing you could change today that will make your character look more like His?***

_____

_____

_____

_____

_____

4

Keep Building

"Therefore everyone who hears these words of mine and puts them into practice is like a wise man who built his house on the rock. The rain came down, the streams rose, and the winds blew and beat against the house; yet, it did not fall, because it had its foundation on the rock."
Matthew 2:24-26

My father has been a contractor for over 45 years and has passed the torch down to my oldest brother who has now been in the business for half of his 46 year-old life. As a young girl, I grew up around nails, sheetrock, particle board, caulk, 2x4's... you name it. Nail guns and the air compressor machine woke me up in the wee hours of the morning before school. The smell of sawdust, tar, and fresh paint are aromas I remember most. An occasional nail in the tire ain't never hurt nobody either, but sure did cause for an expensive bill!

All in all, I wouldn't trade the life I lived (elementary through high school years) for anything. I had the privilege of watching my three older brothers work tirelessly in the summer's heat to pay for their school clothes each year. I watched them carry shingles up a 20 foot ladder and nail each one by hand, while I prayed that they didn't fall and break their backs. As I get older and grow wiser, I'm grateful for my Daddy's sacrifice. He taught me the value of a dollar. His persistence taught me that hard work pays off and that your craft will make room for you if you just keep at it.

As a little girl, when I would watch my Daddy work, I made sure to watch from beginning to end to see how the structure was formed and built, be it a house, business building, or concrete slab. Over time, I realized the process of building a house was not a quick and easy task. It takes time and resources. It takes careful planning. The vision has to be cast. The blueprints have to be drawn up and executed, and the foundation has to be poured correctly for everything else to go up properly, so that when a storm hits, the structure will stand.

I learned that before anything else is built, the foundation must be laid just right. The concrete must dry completely and the homeowners must patiently wait out the process. Otherwise, when the rain and winds come, the house won't last!

Coaches' wives, situations and circumstances will come this year. There may be more losses than wins. The head coach may tear into your husband like nobody's business, but be encouraged. As long as you're built on the solid rock, your family will not be moved! Wins and losses don't, and won't define you, but your character in the midst of adversity will. So, remember the rock that you stand on and trust He won't ever fail you. Keep growing up through every challenge you and your coach may face this season so that you can go up safe, sound, and secure.

Side Note: Ironically enough, John's first collegiate coaching job was at the University of Southern Mississippi. They called their stadium "The Rock". Coincidence? Nah! I knew God was reminding me to depend on Him every time I stepped foot in that stadium! What a promise and an amazing God we get the privilege to serve!

Keep Building

Prayer

❦

God,

Thank you for our biological fathers—those who are in our lives and those who decided to walk away. We know that you, ultimately, will provide all we need in the absence or presence of an earthly father. Thank you for providing what we didn't have or what we missed in the process. Fill the void of every wife that longs to feel the warmth of a father's hug. Repair broken relationships and broken hearts. Thank you for those who stuck around. Thank you, God, for every hail storm, ever thunderstorm, and ever tatter of rain that came at us, but didn't get in us, for we know that when we are built on a strong foundation we can and will stand the test of time. Help us to build our husbands up with our words, in this season, and not tear them down. Thank you for keeping them in your care. God, as they travel to every road game and every home game, surround the highways and airways with your guardian angels. When they're not strong, may we be strong for them. May we encourage and remind our coaches that we are built to last and the process is so much more rewarding when we follow it through to the end… TOGETHER!
What a beautiful structure it shall be.

In Jesus' name,
Amen!

Application & Transformation

Illumination: What are your thoughts concerning this devotional? What is God asking you to believe?

_____

_____

_____

_____

_____

Application: What is God asking you to **DO**?

_____

_____

_____

_____

Transformation: The Holy Spirit has revealed His character to you through this study. **What is one thing you could change today that will make your character look more like His?**

_____

_____

_____

_____

_____

5

Rooftop Runaway

*"In the same way, the tongue is a small thing that makes grand speeches.
But a tiny spark can set a great forest on fire."*
James 3:5 (NLT)

I've been guilty of fussing too much. Saying the wrong things at the wrong times in the wrong way, and ultimately, regretting it when I calmed down and came to my senses. I'm sure you can relate. The reality is, you are human and were born into sin, and things happen. We get out of control. We bark too much with no bite (my husband's words). We say things we want to take back, and we realize, after the fact, that it's too late. We say I'm sorry, but sorry doesn't relieve the sting. Only for a minute, it numbs the sting, but the pain comes back…always. Sometimes even greater!

Ladies, I want you to be mindful of your words during football season, especially, but certainly in every season of your life. Your husband needs your support, not your attitude. He is well aware that you're holding the fort down. He knows you get tired. He knows by your many hints that it's time for a date night, and perhaps he's trying to work that out as soon as he gets a day off, so just be patient. Don't let your emotions run him to the roof. Get control of your emotions; don't let them control you. Football season is but for a moment, so don't look back in December and realize you've torn your family apart in four months. Just like football, the possession of the ball changes constantly, but those who make the right plays when they have the ball are the ones who win.

When you have possession of the ball, be sure to make the right moves. When your husband is home, make sure he wants to be there. Stay focused on the prize. Your marriage, family, and friends will need you long after the time runs out in the fourth quarter. Don't ruin what you have, focusing on what you don't. If your coach hasn't bought you flowers in a while, go by yourself some. If he's like mine, he will ask where they came from and then you can explain that you bought them for yourself because you thought they were beautiful. If he hasn't picked up his belt off the floor in a couple of days, just grab it and throw it in his closet, neatly. (*I said neatly*)

Remember, the person you really want to please is God, and he will make up for everything you think you've lost in this season. Proverbs reminds us that no one wants to be in the house with a fussy, quarrelsome wife. Please don't let that be you!

*"Better to live on the corner of the roof
than share a house with a quarrelsome wife."*
Proverbs 21:9 (NIV)

*"It's better to live alone in the corner of an attic
than with a quarrelsome wife in a lovely home."*
Proverbs 25:24 (NLT)

Rooftop Runaway
Prayer

Dear Lord,

**Keep my mouth from speaking evil, my mind
from thinking evil, and my hands from doing
evil. May my thoughts and my mind operate
in love. May I find comfort in your peace, your
power, and your purpose for my life. Surely, God,
it is not my intention to run my husband on the
roof. Please help me make sure that
that doesn't happen.**

**In Jesus' mighty name,
Amen!**

Application & Transformation

Illumination: What are your thoughts concerning this devotional? What is God asking you to believe?

_____

_____

_____

_____

_____

Application: What is God asking you to **DO**?

_____

_____

_____

_____

_____

Transformation: The Holy Spirit has revealed His character to you through this study. ***What is one thing you could change today that will make your character look more like His?***

_____

_____

_____

_____

_____

6

Stronger Together

*"How good and pleasant it is when God's people live together in
unity! It is like precious oil poured on the head,
running down on the beard...for there the Lord bestows
his blessings, even life forevermore."*
Psalm 133:1-3

As I journey through this purpose pursuit, I've noticed that the
struggle is to finding my place in the midst of it all. I'm well
aware of what my husband has been called to do, but the question
is, what am I supposed to be doing? I know God has plans for me
as well, but what are they? As I sit and ponder these thoughts, I
remember thinking them the most when my husband, John,
was in the NFL. More often than not, I used to be referred to as
John Simon's wife. Then it turned into Coach Simon's wife, and I
remember wanting to be known by my own thing and to be my
own person so very badly! Ultimately, I wanted people to know my

FIRST and last name! I wanted to be important. I wanted to be somebody other than his, whatever. I wanted to be known for my good deeds and my actions and not his touchdowns and his great plays! Oh, and in the earlier days of our courtship, when I was just "the girlfriend" and then the fiancé, those titles were the worst! No one had much respect for the "girlfriend". Those always come and go, is what they all said.

Then God reminded me that when I stood before Him and took those marriage vows, when people knew my name and when they didn't, that I was supposed to smile anyway and keep it moving. And maybe things would turn around. And they did, but not until I embraced who I had become and settled it in my mind that being "John Simon's Wife" was pretty amazing!

Conviction made me go and get my name changed back to Cecelia Michelle Simon. It was originally Cecelia Stroy Simon after we married because I wanted to hold on to my maiden name, just in case. The Holy Spirit chastised me, though, and told me to let go of my past to receive everything he was preparing for me in my future. So, I stood in the Social Security Administration line on that cold winter morning in Dallas, Texas after being married for three years to **reverse the curse.** I was determined to get all that God had for me, and I was adamant about getting out of my own way.

I began to attend John's NFL games whether there was rain, sleet, or snow, or sunshine and stayed there the WHOLE entire four quarters cheering the team to victory, or worst case scenario, encouraging the team to stay in the game despite the point deficit. My focus changed from me to us.

I said all of that to say: God blesses UNITY. He dwells in homes where there is no division and He rests well in married beds where the sheets are undefiled. The scriptures say unity is like precious oil that runs down from the head (or the leader of your home), which is the husband, and onto his beard, and then onto his royal garments. In other words, the blessings never stop. They flow to everyone who is connected to the head, and that means YOU! Don't ever feel like your presence doesn't matter. Don't ever think that you're not important. Don't ever discount who you are and whose you are because no one calls you by your first name. Who cares! I'll be John Simon's wife from now until the day I die as long as we are one.

So, for every occasional meal you host in your home, for every football player that plays with your kids and knocks a hole in your wall, for every football game you sat at and covered yourself and your children with a blanket to fight back the dropping temperatures, and for every time you smiled when someone referred to as Coach So-And-So's Wife and followed it with, "Oh, and what is your name again?"…keep pressing towards the mark. You are somebody because God says so, and when you know your worth, no one can make you feel less than. Remember, UNITY is the best policy.

> *...For this reason a man will leave his father and mother and be united to his wife, and the two will become one flesh.*
> *Matthew 19:5*

Stronger Together

Prayer

⤙

Dear Daddy,

Thank you for reminding us that being married is team work and there is no "I" in it. Thank you for reminding us that it takes selfless acts of sacrifice to make marriage work. Remind us wives that your grace will bind our hearts and minds together if only we would ask you to do it. Thank you that our names are important because you know every strand of hair on our heads and you call us your own. You created us in your image and your likeness and everything you created you said it was good! Whether others know our names or not, may we remember that our relationship with you is most important. Remind us that we play an intricate role in our husbands' success that they need us and we need them. WE are important because we find our self worth in you! Help us to see ourselves like you see us—beautiful, whole, complete, healed, saved, set free, restored, redeemed, and reconciled! And if at any time we forget who we are, remind us whose we are, and that is yours.

In Jesus' name,
Amen!

Application & Transformation

Illumination: What are your thoughts concerning this devotional? What is God asking you to believe?

_____

_____

_____

_____

_____

Application: What is God asking you to **DO**?

_____

_____

_____

_____

_____

Transformation: The Holy Spirit has revealed His character to you through this study. ***What is one thing you could change today that will make your character look more like His?***

_____

_____

_____

_____

_____

7

All of Him, Less of Me

"But the fruit of the Spirit is love, joy, peace, patience, kindness, goodness, faithfulness, gentleness, and self-control. Against such things there is no law."
Galatians 5:22-23

When I got over myself, I realized that my husband needed a clear mind to perform at his best. Although, I wasn't expressing to him how I felt, because we are one, I'm sure he could feel that he didn't have my total support in those early years of his career. I was upset because he was never home. I was jealous because he was going to work and loving what he was doing, and I was a slight bit salty because everything pertaining to the kids and the house lay on my shoulders to handle and take care of. He came home to shower, sleep and leave again.

Sound familiar? Oh, I'm sure. What I learned, however, was that what I do at home is just as important as what he does all day at his office. When we work as a team, our lives are even more fulfilled and favored! So, I pushed my fickle feelings aside and grabbed hold of faith. It caused me to look into my children's eyes and see the blessing in wiping up every spilt cup of milk, every dirty diaper change, and every haul out of town to one of our boys' basketball, baseball, soccer, or football games, alone. God reminded me that before any other team wins, John and I had to win at home and that it started with my attitude about his profession. God informed me that my role in building our team was just as important as my husband, and He promised me that when I got tired, His strength was made perfect in my weakness (2 Corinthians. 12:9). Everything I needed, He would supply. I wonder what would happen if we truly believed that scripture. I wonder what our marriages would be like if we embraced our roles in our coaches' absence without attitude and discouragement.

What I thought the boys and I lacked in the absence of their father, God took up the slack and then some! And He will do the same for you. He is not slack concerning his promises (2Peter 3:9). Whatever He says He will do, you best believe He's gonna do it! His grace is sufficient. His promises are true. Your eyes haven't seen, nor your ears heard, neither has it "entered into the hearts of man," all of the things God has in store for you and your family (1Corinthians. 2:9), but first you've got to seek Him. Second, you've got to sabotage your stinkin' thinkin', and lastly you've got to stop being selfish. When your husband wins, you win, and he needs your full support AND submission so that he can be his best self as a husband, father, provider, and coach.

You are his biggest cheerleader. No other encouragement, from anybody else is better than yours. Stroke his ego and watch his chest poke out. He will begin to do things you've never seen him do before. What others say and feel doesn't matter more to him than how you make him feel. What you think about him and express to him is important. Like me, you can only fake loving this profession for so long before it becomes obvious. You may be hiding your true feelings from your husband, but you're not hiding them from God.

Embrace who you are and the important role you play in building your team. In our house, we call ourselves #TeamSimon. In fact, this is the name we've chosen for our family group text message. When we send or receive a text from one another, the name pops up. We understand that no one wins if we ALL don't win. The boys already know that we represent Christ FIRST, and #TeamSimon second. That means, if Hubs isn't home to take out the trash, I do it. If I have to make up the bed every morning because I'm the last one to get out of it, that's perfectly alright, and if the boys, have to get outside and mow the grass, then that's the slack they take up when Dad's not home.

Whatever works, make it work for **your** team. If you continue to pout and play the victim role in your house because you "feel" like your job is the hardest, then try doing your husband's job for a day. It's not as easy as it looks. Trust that you are right where God has need of you. Take hope in the fact that the deeper the foundation, the taller the building. Remember, you guys are building together in unity and that seasons always change.

When your husband comes home to a clean home (as best you can), a warm meal on the stove (whether he's already eaten at the facility or not), and a peaceful place to rest his head, it brings calmness to his soul. Who knows, he may have just gotten chewed out by the head coach for missing a read, pulled over for speeding on his way home trying to get there before the kids went to bed, or he could be down on himself because his position didn't perform well on film that day at practice.

Ladies, just be patient. Love unconditionally, and bear much fruit. ***His success is nurtured by your support and respect.*** If you are bitter, it is my prayer that God will make you and your marriage better for your good and for His glory.

All of Him, Less of Me

Prayer

~

Dear Jesus,

We know that everything we need you possess. If it's comfort, you can be that. If it's a listening ear, you can be that too. Whatever it is in the absence of our husbands, thank you for providing the need. May we see our marriage and family as a team. When one wins, we all win, and when one loses, we all lose. God, we need each other to survive. May we embrace our roles with courage and tenacity. May we persevere in the face of adverse circumstances. May we have each others' back and be a shoulder to cry on when the world shuts us out. May our houses become homes that possess much love, forgiveness, peace, grace, self-control and mercy, just as you do for us every day. May our lives bear much fruit during the football season and in all seasons.

In Jesus' name,
Amen!

Below are Scriptures for your reflection:

"But he said to me, My grace is sufficient for you, for my power is made perfect in weakness." Therefore I will boast all the more gladly about my weaknesses, so that Christ's power may rest on me.
2Corinthians 12:9 (NIV)

And my God will meet all your needs according to the riches of his glory in Christ Jesus.
Philippians 4:19 (NIV)

God is not man, that he should lie, or a son of man, that he should change his mind. Has he said, and will he not do it? Or has he spoken, and will he not fulfill it?
Numbers 23:19 (ESV)

That is what the Scriptures mean when they say, "No eye has seen, no ear has heard, and no mind has imagined what God has prepared for those who love him.
1Corinthians 2:9 (NLT)

Application & Transformation

Illumination: What are your thoughts concerning this devotional? What is God asking you to believe?

_____

_____

_____

_____

_____

Application: What is God asking you to **DO**?

_____

_____

_____

_____

Transformation: The Holy Spirit has revealed His character to you through this study. ***What is one thing you could change today that will make your character look more like His?***

_____

_____

_____

_____

_____

8

Marriage is Ministry

*"For your creator will be your husband; the Lord of
Heaven's Armies is his name! He is your Redeemer, the
Holy One of Israel, the God of all the Earth. For the Lord
has called you back from your grief - as though you were
a young wife abandoned by her husband, says your God."*
Isaiah 54:5

If after you read this title you said, "No way! I am NOT a preacher.
What is she talking about? My marriage is ministry? Wait. I'm just
trying to get from day to day," then I get it, 'cause guess what? There
was a time in our marriage, over the last 15 years, when I was just
grateful to lie down at night, close my eyes, and say to myself,
***"Yes, we made it through another day without walking out on one
another."***

Many of us, if we would be honest, are whispering the same thoughts, perhaps today. It's not to say that we don't love our husbands. It's just that some days seem harder than others, like: training camp days, recruiting days when he leaves for weeks at a time, and many days in between. It's these days when we begin to question if we are really cut out for this. We may find ourselves saying, Wait, I didn't sign up for this! I didn't know I would be a single parent for so much of the season.

Then reality tells us that God knew exactly what He was doing, and if you believe He orchestrated your marriage and destined for you and your coach to be together, then your marriage has purpose. It is indeed a ministry and you've got to make this confession today: "I'm ALL IN!"

You see, God created your union, as He did mine, to reflect the beauty of His glory. Therefore, His glory is relational and it can most clearly be seen in relationships. The way you treat your spouse, the respect you have for him, the way you submit to him and how you honor him matters. Why? Because your marriage represents Christ and people are watching to see if they want the kind of Jesus that you have. Those who desire marriage are looking at yours to see if it's all that it's chalked up to be.

Dear coaches' wives, if they don't see God in your marriage, they're not going to desire it. When our example is misleading and contradicting, we are responsible. We must make sure that our marriages are a reflection of God's covenant or else we did nothing more than sign a contract on our wedding day.

Ladies, the hardest part about marriage is accepting that neither of you are perfect. Even after the cake has been cut and the last guest has waved goodbye at the reception, the truth of the matter is, that's when the hard work begins. If you're like me, it took some years of trial and error to figure this one out, but the good news is, I didn't have to figure it out alone. God, my FIRST husband, has been there from day one!

When I learned that Jesus should be positioned as my first love, everything about my marriage relationship changed. I realized that everything I did would reflect who Jesus was. So, I started to exercise my daily responsibilities as John's wife in the name of Jesus Christ. My desire to be faithful, submitted, respectful and honorable toward my husband turned into being faithful, submitted, respectful and honorable toward Jesus. In doing so, John was covered!

So, just in case you've been feeling abandoned lately, or you've been grieving the loneliness and absence of your husband during this season, look up. Your creator is your husband and He possesses all you need! Believe it or not, your marriage is ministry, coaches' wives. Others (and God) are watching, and they know if your marriage is indeed fake or led by faith.

Marriage is Ministry

Prayer

◞

Dear God,

To be honest, many of us have no idea what a marriage is supposed to look like. As a result, we are trying to do it on our own. We looked to our parents, and that didn't work. We looked to the romance novels, and those didn't work. We looked to celebrity fantasies, and that didn't work. Now we are looking to YOU, the only one who can sustain our marriage and keep it together. God, teach us how to love one another. Teach us how to put you first in all of our decisions. Give us wisdom to set aside our wants and needs and succumb to each other's needs. God, may we sacrifice for the sake of the covenant we made between you and our spouses so that your name will be glorified in our marriages and in our homes. May we serve one another even if it takes everything we have in us to do so.

In Jesus' name,
Amen!

Application & Transformation

Illumination: What are your thoughts concerning this devotional? What is God asking you to believe?

_____

_____

_____

_____

_____

Application: What is God asking you to **DO**?

_____

_____

_____

_____

_____

Transformation: The Holy Spirit has revealed His character to you through this study. **What is one thing you could change today that will make your character look more like His?**

_____

_____

_____

_____

_____

9

More Than a Person, He's the Promise

"Wives, understand and support your husbands
by submitting to them in ways that honor the Master."
Colossians 3:18 (MSG)

I sat and watched the movie **Drumline** the other day, and the way I view it now has totally changed from the way I viewed it when I first watched it in 2002 when it first debuted in the movie theaters. The rhythms, the sounds, the beats, and the college atmosphere, sparked many memories of my college days. The movie definitely took me on a road trip down memory lane because while at Louisiana Tech University I was only eight miles from the world renown Grambling State University's "The Baddest Band in the Land".

Now that maturity has set in, and the years have gone by since those good ole' Bulldawg days, I understand, in the movie, when

Dr. Lee, the band director, tells Devin, a pretentious percussionist, "You can't lead without following". As much as Devin wanted to be heard, there was so much more for him to learn. There was no doubt that the kid was talented. There was no doubt that he could play some of the other band members, including drum-line's section leader, under the bleachers, but he had to wait his turn.

As the movie progressed, however, I learned that Devin was hiding a secret. The fact that he couldn't read sheet music was jaw dropping! On top of that, his dad had never been a part of his life. He didn't even attend Devin's high school graduation.
As a result of Devin's past, the inevitable happened—his future was affected by it. He didn't know how to follow because he never had a man in his life to lead him. So, he had to learn the hard way. Devin was kicked out of the band, he and Sean, the drum-line's section leader, who Devin had been at odds with throughout the movie, decided that they could do more together than apart. They came to the realization that the division between the two of them was killing the entire team. It wasn't until they came to this truth that things started to get better for the band.

Devin had to submit. He had to honor the authority of the leader of the drum-line despite his quest to be seen, heard, and known.

Regardless of Devin's past pain, the promise was never found in his father being a part of his life. The promise was found in finding purpose throughout the process. After Devin submitted to the call, God qualified him for the blessing! This is true for marriage, as well.

When we as wives submit to our husbands, we allow him to take ownership of the responsibility God placed in him as a man and as the leader of the family. On the other hand, when we fight against our husband's positions in the home the entire house is thrown off course. The sound isn't unified. The rhythm misses beats. The struggle between who's right and who's wrong never ceases to compromise and the family is, negatively, affected by it.

It is our job, wives, to allow our husbands to flourish in their calling to lead. His past failures has nothing to do with his present position. God has placed on the inside of your husband all that he needs to be successful. The team he is employed by will be fine when the team he comes home to submits and supports him as their head coach, not just as a coach's assistant.

The Promise

Prayer

Lord,

Help us to see our husbands as more than just a person, but a prized possession, one that you love and have taken great detail in creating. Help us to see that together we can do so much more than we can apart. We believe your Word. Two is better than one and a threefold cord is not easily broken. May we find you in all of our broken places before we aspire to be anything more than what you have called us to be. Help us fulfill our position and the purpose you have called us to.

In Jesus' name we pray,
Amen!

Application & Transformation

Illumination: What are your thoughts concerning this devotional? What is God asking you to believe?

_____

_____

_____

_____

_____

Application: What is God asking you to **DO**?

_____

_____

_____

_____

Transformation: The Holy Spirit has revealed His character to you through this study. ***What is one thing you could change today that will make your character look more like His?***

_____

_____

_____

_____

_____

10

Grateful for the Love I Know

"If I could speak all the languages of earth and of angels,
but didn't love others, I would only be a noisy gong
or a clanging symbol."
Corinthians 13:1

In this profession it's so easy to envy another marriage or another coach's family's life. From the outside looking in, the view is perfect! The kids are always kept clean and neat. The wife's name brand shoes and petite physique are admirable. It seems that other couples have no problems and their marriages are perfect. Everything is grand! However, looks can be deceiving, as we all know. And what may seem like a fairy tale may not be at all.

Through the years, I've learned to covet my own home, trust in the love that God has given me, and be content with my portion.

God has given me everything I need and he has faithfully and consistently met yours over the years as well. You may not have the best job, be on the best team, or be receiving the best pay, but you have a job, a roof over your head, and you're taking breaths as you read the words on this page. Love is patient in waiting for God's perfect timing. It's not jealous of another man's stuff. It's not boastful or proud of what God has given you. It isn't irritable and it keeps no record of who has the least or the most stuff. (1 Corinthians 13:4-5) Love is being steadfast during transition. It's teaming up to strategize the best play to knock your next business idea out of the park. Love is what you and your husband work hard to keep alive, honor, and maintain.

Therefore, don't make your husband feel less than because you don't have the latest handbag that the wife sitting next to you has. Don't make him feel unappreciated because he's a high school coach and your desire is for him to be a collegiate coach. Don't beat him over the head every day for all the wrong reasons! Love is communication in the midst of a misunderstanding. It's the calm in the midst of the storm. Love is waiting it out one day at a time. It's understanding and recognizing the expression of love, joy, and peace in YOUR home.

The ESV bible translates love in 1 Corinthians 13:7 as bearing and enduring ALL things from beginning to end, while believing and hoping remains your core.

> *Love **bears** all things, <u>believes</u> all things,*
> *<u>hopes</u> all things, **endures** all things.*

In the words of Pastor Hart Ramsey, "If you only love people when they're strong, you don't know what love is. Love can't be celebrated until it responds to weakness."

I am grateful for the love I know. Not like the world gives it. Not like the magazines portray it. Not like the scenes in the movies convey it. I know love like John gives it. Like my heart receives it. Like God intended it for US. Don't just love during the high points, love your coach during the low ones too, and make sounds of harmony everywhere you go… together.

Grateful for the Love I Know

Prayer

Dear God,

Remind us that love isn't like the magazines portray it. It isn't like the scenes in a romantic movie convey it. It isn't gifts, feelings, or a paycheck. Love is a sacrifice, day after day after day.

Thank you, Jesus, for sacrificing your body on the cross for us. It is, and forever will be the ultimate love gift.

In Jesus' name,
Amen!

Application & Transformation

Illumination: What are your thoughts concerning this devotional? What is God asking you to believe?

_____

_____

_____

_____

_____

Application: What is God asking you to **DO**?

_____

_____

_____

_____

_____

Transformation: The Holy Spirit has revealed His character to you through this study. ***What is one thing you could change today that will make your character look more like His?***

_____

_____

_____

_____

_____

Second Quarter:

I Am My Sister's Keeper

We're going to switch gears here a bit from marriage, and address another aspect of this football journey, one that us wives know all too well and the husbands not so much. It's the coaches' wives circle and the gratefulness of being in, or the awkwardness of being left out. Yes, the reality is, there is truth on both ends. Some wives will like who God created you to be, and some of the others will not. The goal, however, is to be on one accord because again, those are the kinds of relationships the Lord will bless, the kinds of teams that our God will smile upon, and the attitudes Jesus will be pleased with.

I'm not saying that, on your team, all of you have to be best friends, but what I am saying is it wouldn't hurt if you at least tried. Stretch out of your comfort zone and into someone else's world. You may learn something you've never known or do something you've never done. It's a great big world out there, and we all need each other's gifts to survive.

1 Corinthians 12:12-27 justifies this truth:

12 Just as a body, though one, has many parts, but all its many parts form one body, so it is with Christ. **13** For we were all baptized by[a] one Spirit so as to form one body—whether Jews or Gentiles, slave or free—and we were all given the one Spirit to drink. **14** Even so the body is not made up of one part but of many. **15** Now if the foot should say, "Because I am not a hand, I do not belong to the body," it would not for that reason stop being part of the body. **16** And if the ear should say, "Because I am not an eye, I do not belong to the body," it would not for that reason stop being part of the body. **17** If the whole body were an eye, where would the sense of hearing be? If the whole body were an ear, where would the sense of smell be? **18** But in fact God has placed the parts in the body, every one of them, just as he wanted them to be. **19** If they were all one part, where would the body be? **20** As it is, there are many parts, but one body. **21** The eye cannot say to the hand, "I don't need you!" And the head cannot say to the feet, "I don't need you!" **22** On the contrary, those parts of the body that seem to be weaker are indispensable, **23** and the parts that we think are less honorable we treat with special honor. And the parts that are unpresentable are treated with special modesty, **24** while our presentable parts need no special treatment. But God has put the body together, giving greater honor to the parts that lacked it, **25** so that there should be no division in the body, but that its parts should have equal concern for each other. **26** If one part suffers, every part suffers with it; if one part is honored, every part rejoices with it. **27** Now you are the body of Christ, and each one of you is a part of it.

11

Your Vibe
Attracts Your Tribe

"But Ruth replied, "Don't ask me to leave you and turn back. Wherever you go, I will go; wherever you live I will live. Your people will be my people, and your God will be my God. Wherever you die, I will die, and there I will be buried. May the Lord punish me severely if I allow anything but death to separate us! When Naomi saw that Ruth was determined to go with her she said nothing more."
Ruth 1:16-18 (NLT)

I am so very blessed by Ruth's loyalty to Naomi. Not only did she leave all that she had to be with her mother-in-law, but she also wouldn't give up on her or her God. Despite all they had been through, Ruth was committed to making sure her mother-in-law was taken care of. The death of their husbands and Naomi's two sons I'm sure shook their core, but the love these two shared sparked a hope that transcended all human understanding. The relationship they established during the hard times caused them to keep pushing in spite of their discouragement and disappointment.

What I love most about this story is that when Ruth and Naomi moved back to Naomi's home country, though Naomi was bitter and had changed her name to Mara, Ruth refused to abandon her mother-in-law's birth name. She refused to let what happened to her become apart of her. She believed in the God that Naomi taught her to believe in and she wasn't letting him go because of a setback. Naomi knew that her mother-in-law was experiencing a season that would one day change.

Ruth remained focused and continued to pursue purpose. She risked her life to go out and find food in a field that didn't belong to her. She became low so that God could bring her high, picking up the leftovers of those who had the right to the harvest. She did this night and day until others in the field started whispering about her. *Who is this girl? Where did she come from? We heard she came with Naomi from Moab. They don't have nothing. They returned empty! Girl, did you hear about it?*

"You know, she's been really faithful in these fields," one worker said. *"She's been working hard from sun up to sun down and she only rested for a few minutes then went back out to pick up behind the other harvesters, again. In fact, she's been picking up behind us all day. Not once has she gotten in our way."*

This story in the Bible reveals Ruth's confidence in God. Although she was in a new place, she didn't let that stop her from focusing on why they were there and what her purpose was in the midst of it all. Ruth knew she had been chosen by God to dwell with her mother-in-Law, Naomi, despite her most recent disbelief. She didn't give up on her purpose. She was destined for her promise.

Question: Are you currently experiencing whispers, unsettling looks, awkward moments around other coaches' wives? Then my suggestion to you is to STAY FOCUSED. God's purpose for you has nothing to do with how anyone else feels about you. If you love God, keep loving God. If they don't, then perhaps your light will shine in their dark places. Just don't get caught up in being "liked" or being popular in the clique or the crowd. People are fickle and their feelings change often, so put your trust and confidence in Christ. He is the ONLY one who promotes you. He is the ONLY ONE who matters. Be sure that you are spending more time concerned about how He feels about you than how they feel about you.

When our husband comes home, they don't want to hear about coaches' wives drama. They have enough drama in the meeting room, alone. Be bigger than that. Be smarter than that. Be better than that. Don't major in the minor. Again, focus. The things of God are so much more important than who rolled their eyes at you, who didn't invite you to their girls outing last season, who didn't tag you in their picture on Facebook or allow you to get into the group photo. If those are their only concerns, then you might want to find a different group of friends anyway. Your promise is greater!

Choose to be around people who will celebrate you, not just tolerate you. Your vibe really does attract your tribe and the grass is not always greener on the other side. If you don't have very many friends, then celebrate a peaceful life. If your phone's not ringing off the hook and you're not receiving text messages every 15 minutes, then rejoice that your life is drama free. Ladies, don't get caught up in numbers or cliques. Be confident in who God created you to be. You are special to Him. You are loved unconditionally by Him, flaws and all!

By the end of the story, Ruth had gained so much more than she had lost, and God wants to do the same for you. Stay in the game, my fellow coach's wife friends. When you're empty—be it friendships, relationships, or love—know that that's when God will fill you up. The content of your character can't be denied. Keep being faithful to God and He will bring you faithful friends.

Your Vibe Attracts Your Tribe

Prayer

Dear God,

Thank you for loving me just the way I am. Thank you for creating me in your image and your likeness. You said in the book of Genesis that everything you created was good. Thank you that I am good—good in my relationship with you, good in my relationship with my husband, and good in my relationship with my family—those things that really matter. Bring people my way who will love you like I love you. Bring people in my life who will stand up and proclaim, "I am a child of God, unashamed and unapologetic." Remind me that if they're not for you, then they aren't for me. May you give me a boldness to serve you and my purpose despite how others feel about me. May I keep my eyes on you at all times and experience your presence even the more as I commit my life to serving you on and off the field. God, may my life give off positive vibes that reflect your character so that I will attract those same types of people to your kingdom. People of substance. People of destiny. People of faith.

In Jesus' name I pray,
Amen!

Application & Transformation

Illumination: What are your thoughts concerning this devotional? What is God asking you to believe?

_____

_____

_____

_____

_____

Application: What is God asking you to **DO**?

_____

_____

_____

_____

Transformation: The Holy Spirit has revealed His character to you through this study. ***What is one thing you could change today that will make your character look more like His?***

_____

_____

_____

_____

_____

12

Her Success Is Not Your Failure

"We are all infected and impure with sin. When we display our righteous deeds, they are nothing but filthy rags. Like autumn leaves, we wither and fall, and our sins sweep us away like the wind."

Isaiah 64:6 (NLT)

New seasons and transitioning to new teams are exciting times! Meeting new coaches' wives, making new friends, and sharing parenting tips is always a plus, but with that comes anxiety, apprehension, and for some, intimidation and rejection.

All mothers think they're doing a great job until they see another mom who has more patience, is slow to speak and quick to listen, and who "appears" to be the perfect example of a super mom, that is until they stop looking from afar and get to know her up close.

Truth is, we all have our moments. Some are better than others, and on our best days, the bible says we are still but filthy rags.

Therefore, don't idolize anyone, and please don't think you're not a good mom just because you watched someone interact with their kid for two seconds and all looked lovely. Don't allow yourself to believe that you're the worst at your job and that that mom should run for PTA president. No! Stop comparing yourself to other women. Learn from them, but don't wish you were them. You don't know their struggle. You don't know what they've gone through to get to where they are. You don't know the turmoil, adversity, and tragedies they had to push through to develop so much patience and joy.

Be content with what's on your plate. The bible says in Philippians 4:11, "I am not saying this because I am in need, for I have learned to be content in whatever circumstances." God gave you what He knew you could handle in whatever season you are in, so trust in that promise. He said He won't leave you nor will He forsake you (Hebrews 13:5). Remind him of that promise, daily, and lean on him. Trust in his timing and stay in your lane. Keep pursing *your* purpose and *your* dreams, and if she has gone where you desire to go, then take her out to lunch and ask her how she got there. See if she will mentor you or give you some tips over coffee, but the worst thing to do is get jealous and start whispering to others about her accomplishments. You won't ever receive your blessing that way. Those are hater characteristics and I'm certain, Sis, that you're not that!

I am reminded of two sisters in the book of Genesis, chapters 29-33, by the names of Leah and Rachel. Both envied and were jealous of one another for the wrong reasons. One was tricked into marrying her husband, and the other was chosen by her husband.

Rachel, the younger sister, appeared to have it all going for her—the good looks and the heart of her husband, but she failed to bear children. Meanwhile, Leah, her older sister, was popping babies out left and right, but Leah didn't have her husband's love. Every day, for more than a decade, each desired what the other had. Envy was knocking at their door steps and both were miserable.

The quarreling, the bickering, the rolling of the eyes, the fighting, the deception, and the strife didn't change the outcome, solve the problem, or get either of them what they desired. By the end of the story, Leah had to find contentment in conceiving six sons and one daughter for her husband, but that still didn't change her relationship with him or the way he felt about her. Likewise, Rachel had to realize that she was on God's timing to conceive a child, and not her own, no matter how hard she tried to make happen what only God could make happen for her and her husband.

Both had to come to terms with the season God had them in and realize their perspective had to change if their situation was ever going to. Success comes from the favor of God, hard work and determination. Failure only comes when you don't try. In this life, before it's all said and done, you will experience both. His timing is perfect. Stay the course. Her success is not your failure, but a beacon of light into your future.

Her Success is Not My Failure

Prayer

Dear God,

Help me to stay focused. You have put on my plate what I have the appetite for. Nothing more and nothing less. Help me to be content with my portion. Remind me that it's insulting to you when I covet what others have instead of being grateful for what you've given me. God, I repent and I refuse to go another day hating my sister for things and stuff that is here today and gone tomorrow. May I set my gaze on eternal things and not the things of this world that are temporary. Thank you for helping me embrace my sister's success and not be envious of her. May you use me to break barriers, build bridges, and tear down walls where hatred, bitterness, and division have taken up residence. God, use me for your glory and to be my girlfriend's biggest cheerleader.

In Jesus' name,
Amen!

Application & Transformation

Illumination: What are your thoughts concerning this devotional? What is God asking you to believe?

_____

_____

_____

_____

_____

Application: What is God asking you to **DO**?

_____

_____

_____

_____

_____

Transformation: The Holy Spirit has revealed His character to you through this study. ***What is one thing you could change today that will make your character look more like His?***

_____

_____

_____

_____

_____

13

Confidence Has
No Competition

"In quietness and confidence shall be your strength."
Isaiah 30:15

I've always struggled with pimples here and there throughout my teens, but when my husband took a coaching position in Arizona, the pimples got worse. I mean there was like a new break out every morning until I finally went to the dermatologist. The diagnosis was adult acne. *"In my 30's?" I asked. "Yes," the doctor replied. "Here's how we are going to combat the break outs."* I was all ears!

The more I noticed the blemishes, the more I felt insecure and ugly, but I would never mention my frustration to my husband. I knew he could see every breakout, but something inside of me wouldn't involve him in my insecure conversations. There was nothing he could do about it anyway. A huge part of me just wanted to protect him from having an opinion that I wouldn't agree with, or a suggestion that I wasn't trying to hear. At best he would reveal what I already knew adding gas to the fire of my already blazing low self-esteem.

Learning to leave him out of those conversations has helped our marriage many days. *"Honey, do I look fat in this dress?"* *"Babe, if I could just have her hair..."* and *"She's so petite and pretty. Wish I looked like that."* Honestly, these are the types of questions and comments your husband doesn't want to hear. If you must, discuss those things with a trusted girlfriend who will be honest in love about what you should change about your appearance, but know that God is in love with all of you. And if truth be told, your husband is too. Don't put him, yourself, or others in a position to respond honestly to a question that you're not ready to hear the answer to.

The dermatologist decided, by the end of our first visit, that giving me a topical medicine wasn't going to get the job done. She insisted two prescriptions that would work together to fight against what was going on on the inside of my body, to change the results on the outside of my body. It took about three to six months before I saw a visible change. Patience and persistence became my greatest assets. Doubt and discouragement had to flee. Although I was looking for a quick fix, my desperate desire to change my appearance could only begin from the inside out. During that time, I had to find my confidence in Him and say to myself what He had already said about me. I had to come to grips with the fact that Jesus' opinion was the only opinion that mattered and doing the work from the inside will always make the outside shine brighter.

Confidence Has No Competition

Prayer

Dear Jesus,

We are who you say we are, and we can do whatever you say we can do. Let our confidence come from the inside out as we get in your presence daily to know and fully understand who we really are in You. Trusting you will teach us about ourselves and remind us that we have been fearfully and wonderfully made. Help us to do the hard work from the inside so that we will see the results on the outside. May we find our confidence in your character, knowing we are your children, and that being content in You is enough.

In Jesus' name,
Amen!

Application & Transformation

Illumination: What are your thoughts concerning this devotional? What is God asking you to believe?

_____

_____

_____

_____

_____

Application: What is God asking you to **DO**?

_____

_____

_____

_____

Transformation: The Holy Spirit has revealed His character to you through this study. **What is one thing you could change today that will make your character look more like His?**

_____

_____

_____

_____

_____

14

Lead With Purpose in Mind

"After the death of Moses, the Lord's servant, the Lord spoke to Joshua, son of Nun, Moses' assistant. He said, "Moses, my servant is dead. Therefore, the time has come for you to lead these people, the Israelites, across the Jordan River into the land I am giving them."
Joshua 1:1-2 (NLT)

Believe it or not, there are people watching your every move. They are looking up to you to make sure you are leading them in the right direction. You are their example, whether you want the responsibility or not. Unfortunately, many of us don't see ourselves as leaders, so we succumb to imitating those we desire to be like, or becoming jealous of those we aspire to be. The truth of the matter is, we all have leadership qualities on the inside of us, but when the rubber meets the road, it's about your commitment to carrying the call out. Will you decide to do the work to become all that God has called you to be, or will you settle for mediocrity?

It wasn't that Joshua was this great human being. It was that this great human being named Jesus chose him to do something that would change the trajectory of a nation. This next level blessing would take bravery and courage. It was a step outside of Joshua's comfort zone. It was going to strip him of the familiarity of the norm. It was not an easy task, but Joshua didn't back down. He didn't tuck his tail and run and hide. Despite the fear and uncertainty, Joshua kept his eye on the prize!

Are you willing to surrender to the life God has called you to lead, or are you okay with preying from afar on the one you envy? Are you just going to settle and shrink back to blend in with the crowd, as to not offend anyone with your Christian life?

Are you okay with closing your mouth to save face when you know what they said and did was wrong? Out of fear, do you just turn the other cheek when you know if your friend continues in that relationship with that person that is not her husband, it will ruin her family? Will you live in fear of what others will say, forever? Will you continue to allow their thoughts and murmurs control your life, or will you do like Joshua and walk out purpose into the unknown with God's hand guiding you every step of the way?

The great thing about Joshua was that he didn't become a leader to be seen or heard. His leadership role had purpose. His purpose was to lead a nation, that had been wandering in the wilderness for 40 years, into a land that was promised to them. He knew he would only succeed if he followed God's every instruction.

Coaches' wives, I believe our plot for desiring to be known is led by the wrong motives. Yes, we all have a leader on the inside of us, but for what reason are you desiring that title? To say you are this or that? To one up your fellow sister? To have a little power and make sure everyone knows it? To be able to do what you want to do and enforce rules on others that you don't follow yourself? I hope not, my friends.

God's grace towards us led him to his death for us to have eternal life. He was not pursuing personal power or status. Perhaps we should re-evaluate our motives, like mentioned before. Are we interested in power or purpose? Success or service? Getting or giving? The reality is, God will only give his blessings to those who can handle giving them away. He will only bless those whose hearts will use those blessings to bless others.

It's important to note that Jesus was made a perfect leader through his suffering. It wasn't until after He died on the cross that He sat at the right hand of the Father, gaining authority over ALL. People who have known pain lead with purpose in mind! Ask God how you can help others through your own personal experiences. That's the sign of a true leader.

I once desired for my husband to be a head coach, but I had to ask myself real questions and then respond with real answers. I learned that I wasn't ready at the time because my motives weren't in the right place.

Coaches' wives, if you desire position for power, status, or money, the bad news is, your talent may take you where your character won't keep you. Be wise in your reasoning. Be kind and considerate when you think of others. Be a leader because you desire to create other leaders. You have it in you, but only if you are willing to allow God to give it to you, to get it *through* you.

God says it this way, "**For what shall it profit a man, if he shall gain the whole world, and lose his own soul.**" (Matthew 8:36 KJV) Also written in Matthew 16:26 and Luke 9:25

Prayer

Dear God,

Thank you for placing a leader on the inside of us, but right now Father, do a CAT Scan on our hearts. What is our reasoning for desiring our husbands to be in big positions, making more money, and having titles attached to their names? If our husbands already hold these positions, search our hearts for the things we've said and done wrong to those we get the privilege to lead every day. If they don't hold this position, remind us that you bless pure hearts. Help us to go to those persons and ask for forgiveness, immediately. God, thank you for the places you've taken us and the positions you've placed us in, but remind us that if you're not getting the glory out of our lives, then it's all for nothing. If we don't have love, the bible says we are nothing. (1Corinthians 13:2) Leaders with no love are nothing. Thank you for this reminder as we all self-evaluate our motives. Thank you for raising up a generation of powerful women of leadership in this industry who have a love for their sisters and a heart to glorify you in all that they say, think, and do. Whether holding a position of leadership or not, may we all use wisdom when making choices and with how we treat others.

In Jesus' name,
Amen!

Application & Transformation

Illumination: What are your thoughts concerning this devotional? What is God asking you to believe?

_____

_____

_____

_____

_____

Application: What is God asking you to **DO**?

_____

_____

_____

_____

Transformation: The Holy Spirit has revealed His character to you through this study. **What is one thing you could change today that will make your character look more like His?**

_____

_____

_____

_____

_____

15

Wise Women Win

"That night God appeared to Solomon and said to him, "Ask for whatever you want me to give to you. Solomon answered, "God you have shown great kindness to David my father and have made me king in this place. Now, Lord God, let your promise to my father David be confirmed, for you have made me king over a people, for who is able to govern this great people of yours? God said to Solomon, "Since this is your heart's desire and you have not asked of wealth, possessions or honor, nor for the death of your enemies, and since you have not asked for a long life but for wisdom and knowledge, govern my people over whom I have made you king, therefore wisdom and knowledge will be given you. And I will also give you wealth, possessions and honor, such as no king who was before you ever had and none after you will."

2 Chronicles 1:7-12

I find these Scriptures very interesting because out of all the things Solomon could have asked for and God would have granted him, he chose **wisdom**. He didn't ask for a better paying job; he didn't ask for his wife to be home more to help him out with the kids; he didn't seek fortune and fame. His desire was the thing that would point him in the right direction for all the other things he may have wanted from God and didn't ask for.

Proverbs 16:16 says, "How much better to get wisdom than gold, to get insight rather than silver." (NIV)

"The one who gets wisdom loves life; the one who cherishes understanding will soon prosper." (Proverbs 19:8 NIV)

"When pride comes then comes disgrace, but with humility comes wisdom." (Proverbs 11:2 NIV)

What we understand here from the wisdom in Proverbs is that regardless of what we are up against, asking God for wisdom in that particular situation will begin to solve the problem. Instead of asking God to remove that situation from us that may temporarily Band-Aid the problem, we should ask Him for wisdom for solutions that will heal the wound.

In a leadership role, as you govern other people in your home as a mother, and in your marriage as a wife, ask God for wisdom to be able to answer hard questions and receive instruction on how to assess and find answers in a challenging situation.

Approach your feelings from now on by asking God for wisdom, then defeat them with your faith. Your current situation will change, but not before you change your mind about your situation. Seek God for the things that will last: love patience, peace, grace, a bridled tongue. Wisdom will give you priceless possessions that money can't buy. The world will give you a defeated perspective. Seek God's infinite wisdom over everything. And in the meantime, just as Jesus did for Solomon, watch him give you everything you didn't ask for, and more!

> *"She opens her mouth with wisdom,*
> *and the teaching of kindness is on her tongue."*
> Proverbs 31:26

Prayer for Wisdom

Dear God,

Thank you for reminding us through the scriptures that wisdom is a precious commodity. Its value is priceless. It would be foolish of us not to ask for it. It would be detrimental to our lives to seek other things over it. Help us to be patient in understanding it. May our lives be preserved by wise choices.

In Jesus' name,
Amen!

Application & Transformation

Illumination: What are your thoughts concerning this devotional? What is God asking you to believe?

_____

_____

_____

_____

_____

Application: What is God asking you to **DO**?

_____

_____

_____

_____

Transformation: The Holy Spirit has revealed His character to you through this study. **What is one thing you could change today that will make your character look more like His?**

_____

_____

_____

_____

_____

16

Girl, Get in the Game!

*"Do you realize that in a race everyone runs,
but only one person gets the prize? So run to win!"*

1 Corinthians 9:24

I was scrolling through Instagram one day and saw this quote by Michael Jordan. It read, "My body could stand the crutches, but my mind couldn't stand the sideline." Simply put: I can bear the pain of brokenness, but what I can't bear is the pain of never playing again. I'm sitting here looking at a game that I was once well able to play in, but my current circumstance has caused a delay in my destiny.

Needless to say, I scrolled past and then back to this quote. I read it again, slowly, and thought to myself, how many times have we allowed our condition to impede our position? To hold us back from doing all that God has called us to do, only to wallow in our self-pity and doubt? To conjure up negative thoughts and assumptions about things that may never happen or come true?

The game, as Michael Jordan witnessed it, was being played right before his eyes, but because of his physicality, he couldn't do anything about it, which is understandable. But how many of us can do something about our situation and we refuse to get back in the game? Has life knocked you down and you can't seem to find the courage to get back up? Are you making excuses in your husband's absence during football season to think of all the reasons why you can't do this and why you can't do that?

I hear complaints like, *I have the kids all day. I can't go back to school! My husband's not home. I can barely get a shower with this newborn, much less try to start a business or volunteer at a local shelter. I don't have time for anything or anyone else.*
And though I get it, and I'm not minimizing your feelings because they are valid, I don't totally agree with them.

Honestly, it has been during football season when I have done my best work! In fact, I type the pages to this devotional on the nights my husband comes home late from the office. I take advantage of the time he is away. In fact, it was during football season, last year, that I started seminary. While he practices and does his daily meetings, I go to school during the day and work on papers at night, after the boys are down, and before he comes home.

I'm not minimizing your responsibilities, ladies. We all have them. But what I am encouraging you to do is not give up because you're waiting on him or others to help you. That help may never come. Don't look back and think, *If I would have started that last year, I would be done by now.* Don't let precious time pass you by. Once it's gone, you cannot and will not be able to get it back. Life will pass you by if you let it. So stop making excuses. Use the football season to work on your goals and your talents while your husband works on his. My husband always says to me, "You don't usually worry about what I'm doing until you don't have anything to do." And he's so right! As long as I am busy doing me, he could be jumping over the moon and I would never know.

Get back in the game, girlfriends. Your team needs your participation to win. You were never meant to sit on the sideline!

> *"Give her of the fruit of her hands,*
> *and let her works praise her in the gates."*
> *Proverbs 31:31*

Girl, Get in the Game!

Prayer

~

Dear God,

Thank you for reminding us that our future is worth fighting for, although, at times, our responsibilities make us feel like what we do from day to day is not important. Thank you for your precious thoughts towards us. You have numbered the hairs on our heads and you know us by name. Dear Jesus, help us to see ourselves like you see us...credible, intelligent, smart, witty, assets not liabilities, women with great talents and gifts, wives of noble character, worth far more than rubies, lacking nothing of value and our husbands have full confidence in us. God, may we bring them good and not evil, all the days of their lives. May we set about our work vigorously, be clothed with strength and dignity, speak with wisdom, and laugh at the days to come because we know that our work is not in vain as long as we receive instruction from you to make our days on this earth productive. May our goal to glorify you in all that we do come to pass.

In Jesus' name,
Amen!

Application & Transformation

Illumination: What are your thoughts concerning this devotional? What is God asking you to believe?

_____
_____
_____
_____
_____

Application: What is God asking you to **DO**?

_____
_____
_____
_____

Transformation: The Holy Spirit has revealed His character to you through this study. ***What is one thing you could change today that will make your character look more like His?***

_____
_____
_____
_____
_____

IT'S HALFTIME!

Perhaps the first half of your game wasn't the best half. You've read these first two weeks of devotionals and you're cringing on your couch. Maybe you got a little side tracked from life's twist and turns. Maybe the ball didn't fall on your playing field the way you expected. Perhaps your team is not having a good year and it's affecting your marriage and your home life. You've said some things you shouldn't have said to your coach in the privacy of your own home and you feel guilty, or not many words are being said at all when hubs comes home and you both say the least to regret saying too much.

You continue on your quest to take care of the kids and the home while keeping a smile on your face when you're around other wives, wondering if they've put their foot in their mouths a couple times before also. You're frustrated, to say the least, and you think to yourself, "Maybe this coaching thing is not all it's cracked up to be." All the while you're trying to keep the peace in your marriage. What you really want to say though is, "I'm losing it. This thing is hard, and I'll trade the money, the long hours, and the late nights for more time with my husband, our children, and less stress!"

I get it. Those are priceless commodities. Peace of mind, less stress, and family time are things money can't buy, but the reality is, that's not reality. You know why? Because I've had this conversation with my husband, and in so many words, this is what he had to say… **"Cecelia, anything worth having is worth fighting for."** Successful CEOs had to miss some parent-teacher conferences and t-ball games to climb the corporate ladder to success, but it all paid off when Dad was promoted and began making enough money to hire an assistant to take on his minor duties so that he can focus on the major responsibilities like being at baptisms and graduations.

John said, "If I had a less stressful job, Bae, such as my own lawn service, I'd still have to go cut people's yards, make phone calls, get up early and make customers happy. I'd have to set my agenda, create my schedule for the week, and make sure our employees are doing their best work. This would take time away from us and our family, too, just like coaching does. A successful customer-satisfactory-business takes time and patience and determination. Just as any job would."

See, my friends, the amenities you currently get to experience are because of the hours and the work your husband puts in. Truth be told, if he didn't spend the time he does in the office, you and your children would be out on the streets or living at less than what your heart desires. So, instead of complaining, let's find this short rest time, during halftime, to regain our composure. To reassess things. To put things back into perspective. To make the main thing, the main thing. Let's stop focusing on the small issues of life, making them bigger than what they are. The more energy you give to a thing, the more it's going to grow. Make sure you are putting your efforts and thoughts into things that matter. Let's regroup and go back out this second half with a renewed strength and a renewed mind. The bible says in Isaiah 40:31 ***"but those who trust in the Lord will find new strength. They will soar high on wings like eagles. They will run and not grow weary. They will walk and not faint."***

Can I be real? The real problem is that you're putting all of your trust in your husband and not God. In fact, you have made him your god and pushed the true and living God to the back burner. You are counting on your husband to fill the voids you are currently experiencing and you're not seeking God for fulfillment. You want more date nights, you want more me time, you want more conversation when he comes home, and he's just not able to give you those things right now. Remember the Day 6 devotional that reminded you that God is your husband? Did you write that scripture on a sticky note and tape it to your bathroom vanity to gaze at every morning? Well, if you didn't, you should. Make it your screen saver on your iPad, computer, or cell phone. Text it to yourself as a daily reminder. Tell your best girlfriend to read it to you when you start to feel lonely and tired. Do whatever you have to do, but don't give up in this season. I know it is a hard one, but you've got another half to go out and give it your best shot. I get it, football wives are some strong women. This task is not given to the weak at heart, but this I know…if God has brought you to it. He will definitely see you through it. The end of your strength is the beginning of His.

The game isn't over until the clock runs out, and when it does, make sure you are pleased with your performance. Your husband needs you. Your team (family) needs you to step it up this next half! They're counting on you to give it all you've got!

Halftime Prayer

Dear God,

May we be the gentle and quiet spirit that our husbands needs in their ears right now. May we be the support that they need to fulfill their destiny. May we not be the voices that push them to the rooftop, but to the mountain top. God, may they hear our voices over the crowd, cheering them on to greatness, encouraging their efforts, and reassuring them that we are their biggest supporters. May our thoughts, words, and actions push them into their purpose. May our love show through action and not just mere words. May our homes be dwelling places where they can rest, relax, recuperate, and get ready for the next play.

In Jesus' name,
Amen!

Third Quarter:

When Passion Meets Purpose

We've been presented with some pretty good offers throughout this journey and when I say offers, I mean contracts. The latest salary appeal beat out my husband's NFL rookie year salary. It most certainly would have accomplished some pretty big dreams and goals for our family, as well as paid some bills and canceled some student loan debt, but surely, by the way I've worded this, you can infer that he turned the offer down.

I remember the phone call, I remember the look on my husband's face, and I remembered him walking out of the hotel room where we were staying to finish the conversation.
Upon his return, I asked him that question we've all asked so many times before, "So, what are you going to do?" His response, "Stay."

It was December. It was cold out. I thought maybe he had the flu or something. A fever, maybe. Because if he wasn't feeling just a tad bit woozy, I was getting a little sick to my stomach. I reminded him of the pay raise he would be receiving if he accepted the job. Then I repeated his response, "Stay," I asked? Yes, "Stay."

My husband was reminded of his passion for the game, but most importantly, that no number could ever interfere with purpose. There was no doubt we were in the state we were supposed to be living in and pursuing the things God had planned for us to do. No dollar amount could ever take destiny's place in our hearts.

That day, I saw how he had grown into the man I had been praying for. Over the next couple of minutes before we headed out for the night, I thanked God quietly, and John, publicly. He needed to know that he had made the right choice and that his wife had been praying that he'd do just that, regardless of what dollar amount this profession presented. As they say, "All money is not good money," and I'm grateful I have a husband who hears from God and acts upon the Holy Spirit's guidance. It makes all the difference in the world.

Now, put me back in the game, Coach! I ain't goin' nowhere!

17

You've Got One Job

*"On the seventh day of the feast, when King Xerxes was in high
spirits because of the wine, he told the seven eunuchs who attended him...to bring Queen Vashti to him with the royal crown
on her head. He wanted the nobles and all the other men to gaze
on her beauty, for she was a very beautiful woman. But when
they conveyed the king's order to queen Vashti, she refused to
come. This made the king furious and he burned with anger."*

Esther 1:10-12 (NLT)

We hear coach's say this a lot to their players. I know my coach has. "You only had one job!" And most times, they're upset because the player blew it! He didn't cover correctly, he didn't block properly, or the kicker missed the field goal to win the game—his ONLY job. And this statement could be applied to so many areas of our lives.

In a marriage, you have an idea of your husband's role as your spouse, as he does of your role as his wife. Most of those ideas were rooted and grounded in what you saw your parents do while growing up. You had an idea, be it right or wrong. Unfortunately, because of our nurturing nature, as women, we get our roles confused sometimes. We don't stay in our lane, and we miss the mark with the only job we are given in marriage.

By becoming their moms, or acting as our husbands' bosses, we compromise our position. The only position we signed up for when we married them was their wives. And we bring all this stress and responsibility on ourselves, trying to be something God never intended for us to be for our husbands. Instead of being the one he longs to come home to, now he's tempted to keep driving past the house. Instead of being the one he finds comfort in, now he's found comfort in a more pleasant conversation on ESPN's Sports Center. Instead of being the one he can tell his secrets and pour his heart out to, he's not sure if he can trust you with his heart anymore. Maybe it's because you've shut him out by shutting down one of his business ideas. Maybe you've scolded him for not taking out the trash. Perhaps, he forgot to pick up bread on his way home from work for the kid's lunch boxes the next morning and now the grocery store is closed. You let him have it when he walks through the door! Whatever it is, it's not worth it! Just ask Queen Vashti.

Many talk about Esther, and they should, but Vashti was the Queen prior to Esther's reign. She was beautiful "eye candy" or the ultimate "trophy wife" for King Xerxes. What she would be in modern days. Nevertheless, he loved her beauty and everything about her, but one day when he called for Queen Vashti, she didn't come. And this was not just any ole' day, but THE DAY when EVERYONE was at the royal palace feasting and having a good time. All the King wanted to do was allow others to lay their eyes on her beauty and she refused. Her refusal to do what he asked (not to mention the disrespect, lack of honor, and lack of love that it displayed to every citizen throughout the empire) made him furious! What a disappointment the King must have felt. Embarrassed much? Absolutely!

As a result, something had to be done. In short, Queen Vashti was forever banished from her royal position and the royal kingdom was no longer hers. She was never to be mentioned or seen again and the King was to choose another Queen who was "more worthy than she" all because she only had one job and she blew it!

Ladies, there is a penalty for your personal fouls towards your husband. Others may not see what you do, but God does. Don't lose your position on the team because you refuse to honor and respect your husband's wishes. Don't wear his "boss pants" and be "Mrs. Bossy Britches" because putting them on will quickly cause you to realize that they are too big for you to handle. It's simple. We have one job. Let's just stay in our lane and handle our position like a lady should. I promise you, despite how it may look, our job is so much easier than theirs. Your husband has a mom; don't be that. He has a boss; don't be that either. Just be his wife. He needs that. And treat your King the way he deserves to be treated.

You've Got One Job

Prayer

~

Dear Jesus,

Help us to just allow our husbands to unwind when they come home from work and be comfortable with just being daddy, husband, and friend. Help us to allow them to just relax, recover, and recuperate from a hard day's work. Remind us as coaches' wives to stay in our lane and remain in our position one that is simple if we see it as such. Help us to not bring more responsibility on ourselves by stepping outside of what we were created to be and do. Help us to allow our husbands to make mistakes. Help us to encourage their endeavors and speak life into their dreams, goals and plans. May they find rest for their weary souls in the comfort of the place they call home.

In Jesus' name,
Amen!

Application & Transformation

Illumination: What are your thoughts concerning this devotional? What is God asking you to believe?

_____

_____

_____

_____

_____

Application: What is God asking you to **DO**?

_____

_____

_____

_____

Transformation: The Holy Spirit has revealed His character to you through this study. **What is one thing you could change today that will make your character look more like His?**

_____

_____

_____

_____

_____

18

The Most Important Play is Your Next One

"Your name will no longer be Jacob," the man told him. "From now on you will be called Israel, because you have fought with God and with men and have won."

Genesis 32:28 (NLT)

Some days just don't go as planned. The goal was to go to the gym today, but it didn't happen. You thought you would have time to cook dinner, but the time just got by you. More than your share of phone calls came your way and threw your whole day off. Your son got sick and threw up four times before sunrise. I get it. Been there! So what do you do when today's to-do list doesn't get met? How do you handle life's surprises?

You get back up and try again the next day! You do like Jacob did and you wrestle with that thing that is trying to defeat you until you defeat it! Don't you dare wallow in self-pity when you don't sell your house in record breaking time or get that blog finished before the holidays. Don't you dare give up the fight. This obstacle didn't come to destroy you. It has come to humble you, to remind you to pray, and to remind you to never give up! It has to show you that apart from God you can do nothing. It has to remind you of your destiny, and that it's going to be a fight to get there, but that when you do, it's going to be worth it.

Your best play is your next play. It's not the one that just pushed you back ten yards, but the one that is going to push you forward and cause you to gain so many yards if you keep pressing forward, because the secret to the fight is; it's already fixed! You've already won! The key is to keep fighting until you receive your reward. The good news is that it's closer than you think.

I heard a story one time and the story teller posed the question, *"If you knew that you would win by outlasting your opponent by five more measly minutes, would you do it?"* I'm certain your answer is yes! The problem is, we don't always know when that last five minutes will come. No one rings a bell. An alarm doesn't go off, and no one alerts you to tell you that there are five minutes left in the fight. But if we keep this winning attitude and decide that when we get tired we will just give ourselves another five minutes to keep going, we will outlast our opponent.

Another five more minutes to round the corner home after a three mile run. Another five minutes on that elliptical of death. Another five minutes praying, or another five minutes conversing with your children at dinner. I wonder what would change? I wonder what life would be like if you didn't give up? My biggest fear is being right here next year because I put more thought into what was rather than what shall be. I hope that's not your biggest fear too. Keep wrestling, my friends, until you win!

Your Most Important Play

Prayer

~

Dear God,

More than being reminded of our past losses, help us to focus on our future wins. What's more important is giving our energy to what is instead of what was. May our next play be our very best play. Who knows? Five more minutes of fight may deem us champions.

In Jesus' name,
Amen!

Application & Transformation

Illumination: What are your thoughts concerning this devotional? What is God asking you to believe?

_____

_____

_____

_____

_____

Application: What is God asking you to **DO**?

_____

_____

_____

_____

Transformation: The Holy Spirit has revealed His character to you through this study. **What is one thing you could change today that will make your character look more like His?**

_____

_____

_____

_____

_____

19

Play from the "W"

*"Nay, in all these things we are more than conquerors
through him that loved us."*
Romans 8:37 (KJV)

By now you should be accustomed to the rules in football like what causes a penalty or lost yardage, and what can cause you to totally be thrown out of the game. My suggestion; make adjustments going into the second half and don't fret over what has already been done. You can't change the past, but you haven't run out of time to fix the mistakes in your future. Another major perspective shift would be to play *from* the WIN and not *for* it from now on.

You are already victorious, so walk in it and act like it, and not when you receive the victory, but before. See, winning is a mindset. It's a lifestyle. It's a habit, and when you already know you possess it, you don't just settle for losing and you don't even consider it. Losing is not an option. It's not in your vocabulary and it's not in your house. As a believer and a coach's wife, you must take on this attitude from this day forward. The bible says you are more than a conqueror, which means you have exceeded winning. You are beyond that!

So speak positive words over every area of your life. Think winning and speak winning all day, every day. Proverbs 18:21 tells us that life and death is in the power of our own tongues. Every single day we wake up, we can choose to speak defeat or we can choose to speak victory in our marriages, in our homes, over our families, and in the work place. It's up to us.

If you were once considering walking away from your marriage because you are tired, don't anymore! Begin to speak life over your husband, his work environment, and your home. Pray over his side of the bed. Write scriptures in his shoes (I did!) and leave little encouraging cards in the driver's seat of his car. Send sweet little text messages (with lots of heart emojis) throughout the day to remind him that you appreciate his sacrifice. He may or may not respond, but I promise you he will read and see your messages, and I'm certain it will make him smile. Galatians 6:7 says, "Do not be deceived: God cannot be mocked. A man reaps what he sows." Therefore, sow love, sow kindness, sow gentleness, sow patience, and sow self-control, and watch God bring a harvest into your house because you didn't give up on sowing seeds of greatness into your husband when times got hard. Don't go into this thing expecting to win. You've already received the victory. Now walk in it!

Play from the W

Prayer

*Dear God,
It is in you we find our confidence. It is in you we find our strength. May we wake up with a winning attitude and may it contagiously rub off on everyone we meet. God, may we never give up on fighting for our families and our marriages. May we contend until we win.*

*In Jesus' name,
Amen!*

Application & Transformation

Illumination: What are your thoughts concerning this devotional? What is God asking you to believe?

_____

_____

_____

_____

_____

Application: What is God asking you to **DO**?

_____

_____

_____

_____

Transformation: The Holy Spirit has revealed His character to you through this study. **What is one thing you could change today that will make your character look more like His?**

_____

_____

_____

_____

_____

_____

20

"Don't Outrun Your Coverage"

- Pastor Darryl Morrison

"So be truly glad. There is wonderful joy ahead, even though you have to endure many trials for a little while.
These trials will show that your faith is genuine.
It is being tested as a fire test and purifies gold..."
1 Peter 1:6 NLT

As I began writing this devotional, I also decided to start a graduate program in Biblical and Theological Studies at Phoenix Seminary. Even though I took this extra responsibility on, laundry didn't stop needing washing and folding. Dinner didn't cease to need preparation, and the many responsibilities that I take on everyday as a mother and wife didn't come to a halt because of this commitment. Floors still got dirty, so mopping was in order. Emails were delivered to my inbox that warranted a response. Due dates for the boys' social studies projects alerted my agenda, and the list goes on and on.

In the midst of it all, I thought that going to seminary would equate to spending time with God. I quickly found out that's not so! Although I write papers about scripture, watch lectures, and study the bible every day, all day, it seems, those activities can't and won't suffice as it relates to my personal time with Jesus. I found myself anxious, irritable, quick with words, and worrying. I was without love, grace, and devotion to my Savior and my family.

I wonder if you know what I mean. I wonder if the cares of this world are weighing you down at this very moment. I hope, if that is the case, that this devotional is giving you hope again in the promises of God. As we are in the second half of this game called life, don't outrun your coverage. There is peace in the presence of God. You're safe when you allow Him to go ahead of you. If you try to do it all on your own, you will fail. The test is building character. It is making a stronger, better, wiser version of you. This season in your life is refining you and establishing your faith. God desires to know that through this process, your faith truly is genuine. For we all know, that real character is seen through adversity.

So, perhaps the first half wasn't all you thought it was cracked up to be. You did some things on your own and realized God wasn't in them. As a result, those things didn't work out like you had originally planned. That's okay. Repent and go back to the drawing board. This time, with God in mind.

As I type, I am reminded of our last two games where we've gone into halftime holding the losing end of the stick. Nevertheless, after readjusting our game strategy in those vital moments, we had to take a break. Our team came back out after halftime and took home the high end of the scoreboard. It's never where you start, my friends. It's ALWAYS where you finish. So, finish with God. Don't try to get ahead and outrun him. Your promise is definite. It WILL come in its perfect timing. Don't even try to rush the process. Just stay faithful to what God has called you to in this season. There is preparation right smack dab in the middle of your pain, but the process is the prerequisite to your promise! Don't chase after the promise. Chase after God's presence. It is then when God will settle your heart and your mind. It is there where you will find contentment.

Don't Outrun Your Coverage

Prayer

Dear God,

Teach us not to get ahead of you. You are our covering and our defense. We must allow you to lead so that you will shield us from the fiery darts of the evil one. May we run, but always behind you and not out in front. We need your wisdom and guidance to lead the way.

In Jesus' name,
Amen!

Application & Transformation

Illumination: What are your thoughts concerning this devotional? What is God asking you to believe?

_____
_____
_____
_____
_____

Application: What is God asking you to **DO**?

_____
_____
_____
_____

Transformation: The Holy Spirit has revealed His character to you through this study. ***What is one thing you could change today that will make your character look more like His?***

_____
_____
_____
_____
_____

21

Faith and Football

"Not that I am speaking of being in need,
for I have learned in whatever situation I am to be content."
Philippians 4:11 (ESV)

The other day I realized I hadn't checked my bank account in a couple of weeks after depositing a significant amount of money. After checking it and going through my statement to make sure all was there, I thought to myself, *"Why did it take you so long to check back?"* I thought, any fraudulent activity could have happened and I wouldn't have known anything about it. Then God said, so softly, *"It is because what you deposited you believed would be in your account whenever you came back to it."*

Truth is, I never worried. I never doubted. I never second guessed it. I trusted that when I went back to my account what I put in would still be there. I wonder what would happen if we had those same thoughts about God, that whatever He placed on the inside of us is enough to get the job done. We don't have to worry. We don't have to fret. We don't have to fear. We just simply have to trust and have faith that whatever God tells us to do, when it is our time, all we have to do is check with ourselves to pull out of ourselves what is needed at that time to accomplish the goal.

Ladies, I'm praying we get to this point. I'm hoping that God kind of faith becomes so loud in our ears that it drowns out every doubt and every fear we might have about reaching our destiny. I'm praying, even during football season, that we are making deposits that will be there when we need them. In other words, give what you desire to have. Sow seed where you would like to reap a harvest. If it's love, give love unconditionally. If it's friendship, you must first show yourself friendly. If it's a financial blessing and what you have isn't enough to meet your need, then it's your seed. Sow it into a charity, ministry, or person that is doing what you would like to do. Bless and, encourage them and God will honor your sacrifice.

You can't draw where there haven't been any deposits. If you continue to receive where you have not given, you will always come up empty handed, but when you make a deposit, walk away. Don't hover over your seed. Pray over it, and every now and again you might have to water it with some tears, but don't give up on it. Watch God do His work and just like me, don't sweat the small stuff. If you've made a deposit in your marriage, then keep it moving. You don't have to keep checking back to make sure your husband saw what you did for him. In due time, you will reap the reward of your kind gesture. Have an attitude of gratitude, come what may.

What is there will be there when you need it. The same goes for your husband. Whatever his heart's desire is, y'all talk about it and pray that it's in God's will for his life and for your family and begin to sow seed in that area. If he wants to go to the next level in coaching, pray and be content with where you are. If he desires to be a head coach one day, pray and be content as a position coach until God opens that door. God is maturing you in this season for your next one, but it won't come without contentment and sacrifice. The Bible says in Luke 6:38, "Give and it shall be given unto you. Good measure, pressed down, shaken together, running over, will be put into your lap. For with the measure you use will be measured back to you." (ESV)

And here's another truth to meditate on throughout your day.

Philippians 4:6 *"Do not be anxious about anything, but in every situation, by prayer and petition, with thanksgiving, present your request to God. And the peace of God, which transcends all understanding, will guard your hearts and your minds in Christ Jesus." (NIV)*

Coaches's wives, make deposits and trust they will be there when you need them, but don't expect to receive where you have not given.

Faith and Football

Prayer

Dear God,

Don't let our plans for our lives rush yours. You have already drawn up the blueprint and you know what's best. What we think we can handle in this season, perhaps we can't. Don't give us anything that will destroy us. Mature in us a heart to receive what you have for us in your perfect and precious timing. Until then, may we be content in what our present deposits possess.

In Jesus' name,
Amen!

Application & Transformation

Illumination: What are your thoughts concerning this devotional? What is God asking you to believe?

_____

_____

_____

_____

_____

Application: What is God asking you to **DO**?

_____

_____

_____

_____

Transformation: The Holy Spirit has revealed His character to you through this study. ***What is one thing you could change today that will make your character look more like His?***

_____

_____

_____

_____

_____

22

My Game, His Glory

"Work willingly at whatever you do,
as though you were working for the Lord, rather than for people.

Colossians 3:23 (NLT)

There was a time in my marriage when I wanted a pat on the back for everything I did. I wanted my husband to notice the bed was made, the dishes were washed, and the refrigerator was stocked. I wanted him to not just notice I was with the kids all day, but also to acknowledge it. If he didn't say anything I would be disappointed. When my husband didn't say anything about what I had done throughout the day, I would get upset and maybe those things wouldn't get done the following day. Attitude! Then one day I realized that I was doing all of that for his praise and not for God's praise. I quickly began to understand that God wasn't cool with that and He was the only one I should have been trying to please.

I knew something had to change. I remembered during marriage counseling, my college ministry pastor would always say, "No expectations, no disappointments." I started to say it too. I didn't really comprehend it then, but I learned what it meant early in my marriage. We should have expectations for our mate, like, him being the provider and the leader of the home, and loving you in sickness and in health, 'til death do you part. Those things, of course. But when your expectations aren't reasonable, and you start looking to your husband for your happiness, your reward, or for that pat on the back, that is when you get what you are looking for—disappointment.

The Message Bible says in Matthew 6:

The World Is Not a Stage

2-4 "When you do something for someone else, don't call attention to yourself. You've seen them in action, I'm sure—'playactors' I call them—treating prayer meeting and street corner alike as a stage, acting compassionate as long as someone is watching, playing to the crowds. They get applause, true, but that's all they get. When you help someone out, don't think about how it looks. Just do it—quietly and unobtrusively. That is the way your God, who conceived you in love, working behind the scenes, helps you out.

Isn't this a slap in the face? Geesh!

If your husband notices the mopped floors today, great! If he doesn't, maybe he will tomorrow. If he doesn't ever, remember you don't want his praise more than you want God's presence. Allow him to relax. *The world is not a stage* and you're not *acting* as his wife. He chose you. Therefore, you ARE his wife. You are a team. His win is your win, so perform behind the scenes so that if only God sees your performance, you are content with His applause and His applause only. You CAN expect Jesus to NEVER disappoint.

The Message passage in Matthew, 6:1 explains it like this: "Be especially careful when you are trying to be good so that you don't make a performance out of it. It might be good theater, but the God who made you won't be applauding."

"Good theater." HA! God certainly has a sense of humor, doesn't He?

My Game His Glory

Prayer

Dear God,

There are times when I want my efforts to be acknowledged. It's just the human side of me, but please remind me when what I do isn't rewarded that that's okay. You don't miss a thing, and at the appointed time, when you are ready, you will make sure I receive the blessing you have set aside for my obedience.

Thank you in advance.

In Jesus' name,
Amen!

Application & Transformation

Illumination: What are your thoughts concerning this devotional? What is God asking you to believe?

_____

_____

_____

_____

_____

Application: What is God asking you to **DO**?

_____

_____

_____

_____

_____

Transformation: The Holy Spirit has revealed His character to you through this study. ***What is one thing you could change today that will make your character look more like His?***

_____

_____

_____

_____

_____

23

The Blessing
Is in the Breaking

"...to grant to those who mourn in Zion - to give them a beautiful headdress instead of ashes, the oil of gladness instead of mourning, the garment of praise instead of a faint spirit; that they may be called oaks of righteousness, the planting of the Lord, that he may be glorified."
Isaiah 61:3

Growing up I was told never to break a mirror. I'm sure many of you reading this were too. You were told that breaking a mirror would give you seven years of bad luck so be careful around them, right? As I got older, and after breaking a couple, I realized that that was a myth. It sounded good, but it just wasn't true. The seven years of bad luck never happened to me. And since I've found this to be a fib, my perspective in my adult years has changed concerning this once terrifying lie.

Instead, I've learned that, when you drop a glass or any such material on a hard surface, that object shatters into what seems to be a million pieces. Days later you find pieces that slid under the cabinet or in the corner. While we try to sweep up and meticulously gather each itty bitty piece, sometimes we just don't get them all and bare feet suffer the consequences. Just ask my husband who came to visit me in my apartment in college and kicked a brown paper bag that had several broken pieces of glass in it. Hmmmm…yeah, he had to get stitches and I had to watch the painful process while feeling guilty about it. We made the news. Well, let's just say I made the local news in our college town. As if that wasn't bad enough Tech had a big game coming up that weekend and the "girlfriend" wasn't putting her best foot forward. (No pun intended.)

Being broken, though, actually wasn't a bad thing for my husband. He didn't miss a beat in that game and went on to play in the NFL. Similarly, Jesus was broken and beaten for our sins. He died on an old rugged cross for our salvation, was buried in a tomb, and on the third day, He rose with all power in his hands. He now sits at the right hand of the Father, petitioning on our behalf as the savior of the world.

I know brokenness doesn't always seem beautiful when you are in the thick of it, but there are lessons you learn during trying times that only such adversity can teach you. Marriages stand taller after they've been pushed around a bit. Relationships can weather the storm when rain has beat on their foundation some, and families know how to survive through tough circumstances after sticking together through rough waters.

I don't know about your current issue, but I just wanted to encourage you that you will come out on the other side if you just hold on. The beauty from your broken pieces will be put back together again and the pain will paint a gorgeous picture for all the world to see!

The Blessing is in the Breaking

Prayer

◠

Dear Jesus,

Sometimes it's hard to see the end from the beginning, or the light at the end of the tunnel, but I know a new day is dawning. I trust that you know what's best for me and what I am capable of handling. When the weight gets too heavy for me to carry, I believe you will take up the weight of my load. In the meantime, give me the strength to keep pressing despite this heaviness I am experiencing.

In Jesus' name,
Amen!

Application & Transformation

Illumination: What are your thoughts concerning this devotional? What is God asking you to believe?

_____

_____

_____

_____

_____

Application: What is God asking you to **DO**?

_____

_____

_____

_____

Transformation: The Holy Spirit has revealed His character to you through this study. ***What is one thing you could change today that will make your character look more like His?***

_____

_____

_____

_____

_____

_____

24

Huddles and Heels

"The Lord said, Go out and stand on the mountain in the presence of the Lord, for the Lord is about to pass by." Then a great and powerful wind tore the mountains apart and shattered the rocks before the Lord, but the Lord was not in the wind. After the wind there was an earthquake, but the Lord was not in the earthquake. After the earthquake came a fire, but the Lord was not in the fire. And after the fire came a gentle whisper. When Elijah heard it, he pulled his cloak over his face and went out and stood at the mouth of the cave."
1 Kings 19: 11-13 (NIV)

Life is busy. Boy, do I know it. Some things on the to-do list get crossed out throughout your day, and some things just have to wait. Being a mom, a wife AND a coach's wife, and all the other hats we wear and switch out throughout the day can be challenging. I mean it can be down right exhausting! And then God whispers and reminds us that we will get tired in our own strength and we will want to quit and give up in our own strength, but when we renew our strength in His Word and spend time with Him in Bible study and prayer, He refreshes and renews our spirit.

Like a huddle in a football game where the quarterback has to gather the team to call a play or readjust the lineup, such is life. Sometimes we have to call a time out and get it together. Many times we have to huddle up and redefine our goals and have those hard conversations with ourselves about what's most important. We have to regroup. We have to prioritize. We have to find clarity and the huddling helps us think clearly because chaos just won't allow us to do that. In the circle, you get to strategize and take a couple of deep breaths. You get your wind back for the next drive down the field. There's a moment of rest. A moment of grace. A moment where nothing else matters but the voice you hear in that space. That circle. The circle that is never meant to be broken. The protection of it keeps the enemy out.

The person who leads in the circle is talking and you're trying your best to drown out the noise of the crowd to hear the next play…the play that will get you closer to the goal line and the winning touchdown…the play that will take you closer to your destiny.

In life, that voice is God's voice. He wants you to huddle with Him so that His voice becomes the loudest in your ear. He wants you to stop everything you are doing and hear what He has to say so that your next play will be your best play! Just like players on a team who closely gather in the middle of the field so that the opposing team doesn't hear their plan to be victorious, God wants you to do the same.

When you carve out time in your day for Him for five, ten, fifteen, maybe even twenty minutes a day, He rebukes the devour for your sake. He wraps you so tight in His arms and whispers sweet secrets in your ear that the enemy can't even begin to figure out. That space is between you and God. Satan isn't invited.

I encourage you today to take time and huddle up with your Creator, Savior, and Lord. He's the only one who knows the intricate parts of you. He is the only one who can help you move forward. Stop everything you're doing and follow His lead. Your next play is depending on it!

Huddle and Heels

Prayer

Dear God,

Out of all the things we could long for in this world, make our hearts desire to long for you. We were created to love and commune with you; therefore, that desire to be in your presence won't go away unless we get there. That void we often feel is because we try to ignore the call, but it just lingers. Help us to be instant in obedience. Help us to seek you first. You've promised to add everything else we might need. May we be intimate with you on a daily basis. May our souls long to communicate with you in prayer. May our hearts be in tune with your voice. May we find time to be still in your presence. Thank you for choosing us. Thank you for your whispers. We can't do life without them.

In Jesus' name,
Amen!

Application & Transformation

Illumination: What are your thoughts concerning this devotional? What is God asking you to believe?

_____

_____

_____

_____

_____

Application: What is God asking you to **DO**?

_____

_____

_____

_____

Transformation: The Holy Spirit has revealed His character to you through this study. ***What is one thing you could change today that will make your character look more like His?***

_____

_____

_____

_____

_____

25

Grace Collision

*"And after you have suffered a little while, the God of all grace,
who has called you to his eternal glory in Christ, will himself restore,
confirm, strengthen, and establish you."*
1Peter 5:10

When my husband played running back in the NFL, I would cringe every time the ball was handed off to him. The anxiety and the stress haunted me. My whole body would tighten as he ran through those tight little holes. My hope was that he came out on the other side in one piece. Some days he did, and some days he didn't. When he got banged up, he would lay there, and eventually he would gather up enough strength to get up and walk off the field, carrying the weight of the pain with him. The sideline was where he recovered. It was his safe place out of harm's way. It was where I felt the safest for him. Eventually, he would have to take another rep and succeed in another play designed specifically for his skill set. The game must go on, and as my two sons and I traveled to the last home game of the season in 2016 where my husband coached, this too became our story.

I was sitting at the stop sign waiting for the east and west bound traffic to cease. At that time all I could think about was getting those, Khaki pants—the pants that he had called about thirty minutes before—to my coach before the start of the game. He needed them and I was responsible for getting this important piece of fabric to him before kickoff. All was clear as I began to pull out into the four crossing lanes. The sun brightly painted the sky as it was going down in the late evening. Everything was good until I felt the side of my truck take a hit. The air bags deployed. My heart immediately dropped to my stomach. I looked back, through the smoke, to see if the boys were okay. Our oldest baby screamed. I was trying to process what had just happened! I never saw the silver car in the distance. It hit just two inches from where our oldest son was sitting. The impact was so hard it knocked the front tire off of our truck. The boys and I couldn't move. Life stood still for just a moment. I had completely forgotten about the pants!

Sometimes life is unsure. We don't always know the plan. God doesn't give us the blueprint for every win and every loss. Many would think that it would be easier to take a blow when you know it's coming, but I beg to differ. Tensing up doesn't promise the pain will diminish in strength. Just as I would close my eyes and hate to watch my then fiance' slide through those holes with the ball, I would also miss the beauty of his foot work, his technique that was timed so perfectly, and the touchdown that followed the punishment it took to get there.

As we have come to know, pain is only temporary. When what you are "growing" through is over, God promises to **restore** what was lost, **confirm** your footing, **strengthen** your heart for what's ahead, and **establish** His purpose for your life (1Peter 5:10).

I don't know how you feel about it, but I'm most grateful for that promise. Your current situation may not make sense at the moment, but keep pushing through the crowd. You'll find a hole and all that your eyes will see is the end zone, but pain sometimes is the prerequisite to His purpose for your life.

Grace Collision

Prayer

⌒

Dear God,
Thank you for grace. Those moments when pain
stings, your promise is always near. Help us to
trust in your perfect timing for our lives. Though
it hurts, we can trust that you are a healer.

In Jesus' name,
Amen!

Application & Transformation

Illumination: What are your thoughts concerning this devotional? What is God asking you to believe?

_____

_____

_____

_____

_____

Application: What is God asking you to **DO**?

_____

_____

_____

_____

Transformation: The Holy Spirit has revealed His character to you through this study. ***What is one thing you could change today that will make your character look more like His?***

_____

_____

_____

_____

_____

26

UnHappy Holidays

*"Always be joyful. Never stop praying. Be thankful in all circum-
stances, for this is God's will for you who belong to Christ Jesus."*
1Thessalonians 5:18

Who doesn't love the smell of the holidays? I mean we wait all year for the sweet smell of Honey Baked ham, pine needles, the toasty smell of nutmeg, cinnamon, and spices for the perfect homemade sweet potato pie. And nothing…I mean no-thing tops MY mama's cornbread dressing when the sage has been carefully measured and dashed in with love. It brightens the whole house with the smell of Thanksgiving.

Then comes Christmas. Houses are adorned with crystal clear lights that illuminate the neighborhood. Strands of green, red, and white bows, wrapping paper, and tape makes that gift attractive to the smallest little eyes, as it's neatly placed under the tree in the perfect spot. And those beautiful dark red cherry cheesecakes are stacked high in the fridge so everyone gets their fill. Those were the days. Life was simple.

And then I fell in love with a football player, we got married, and one morning I woke up at a Hilton Resort in Tucson, AZ on Thanksgiving and the Omni Hotel in Dallas, TX on Christmas day. That's when reality set in. Life's traditions turned into the tragedy, or should I say the truth, of my now.

My perspective changed. I had to find a way to make things work. I had to figure it out the best way I knew how. I learned to love the life I live and make the best of all situations. I thanked God that even though the circumstances were not "normal", I was yet grateful that my family was all together in one place. I became exceedingly grateful for life, and not the things that this life brings. I realized in these moments that stability is found in God and not a date on a calendar because events are always "subject to change" in this profession. The one person, however, who is sure to remain consistent is God. He is the same yesterday, today, and forever (Hebrews 13:8). If He said it, He's going to do it. If He promised, it WILL come to pass.

Know that, God never intended for your happiness to be found in a holiday or in your husband. Life is not "normal" as a coaches' wife. So, if you've agreed to this life, fasten your seat belt and enjoy the ride. There will be turbulence, bumps, and bruises along the way, but know this—when you put your trust in Jesus, you will make it to your destination safely, and it will be up to you to find joy wherever you land whenever you get there. Your happiness will always be found IN you, not in the things going on around you. Stay the course, my friends. Happiness in the holidays are found from the happiness you have within.

UnHappy Holidays

Prayer

~

Dear Jesus,

Holidays can get a little hectic. Sounds and smells remind us of the "good ole' days", but we have to grow up. We have to mature. We have to find you in the midst of what we want to remain familiar forever. You are the only stability in our lives. As coaches' wives, may we be reminded, when life gets a little unfamiliar, that you are the only one who remains the same. May we find hope in the holiness of being your child.

In Jesus' name,
Amen!

Application & Transformation

Illumination: What are your thoughts concerning this devotional? What is God asking you to believe?

_____

_____

_____

_____

_____

Application: What is God asking you to **DO**?

_____

_____

_____

_____

Transformation: The Holy Spirit has revealed His character to you through this study. ***What is one thing you could change today that will make your character look more like His?***

_____

_____

_____

_____

_____

Fourth Quarter:

Bowl or Bust?

Around this time the season is usually coming to a close. Your coach's team has either won enough games in the regular season to ensure your spot in a bowl game in post season, or your coach will be joining your family for more dinners by the end of November. Perhaps, you are in a panic. Your head coach was notified before the beginning of the year that if he doesn't win a certain amount of games, he will be fired, or chances are, the fate of your next job could end up going either way. I've been there on both ends of the stick—when the season left us without a job because of the losses, and when we had a winning season. The search for my husband's next job still happened though.

Truth is, if you rely on this profession to dictate your happiness, you will lose every time in the game of life. Your children will lose and your marriage will lose, but on the flip side, if you trust God and allow His path to direct your next move, the sky is limitless for you and everything connected to you.

Be encouraged today in whatever state you are in. God will never leave you nor forsake you (Hebrews 13:5). He promises that "The steps of a good man are ordered by the Lord, And He delights in his way. Though he fall, he shall not be utterly cast down; For the Lord upholds him with his hand" (Psalms 37:23-24).

You can trust the word of God to be true. Lean on it and not your own understanding. This profession is not logical. It's spiritual. Rely on the Holy Spirit and ask for wisdom wherever this journey will take you. It's definitely not the end. It is only the beginning.

27

Wins and Losses Share the Same Locker Room

*"We are hard pressed on every side, but not crushed; perplexed,
but no in despair; persecuted, but not abandoned; struck down, but
not destroyed. We always carry around in our bodies the death of
Jesus, so the the life of Jesus may also be revealed in our body."*
2 Corinthians 4:7-10

As a woman, I've always wondered about a guys' locker room. I have questions like, does it really smell that bad? Do the guys really walk around naked in front of each other (just sayin')? Where does athlete's foot come from in there? How'd he shower so fast after the game? And then I peeped in one day (okay, I admit it's hard not to when you're a coach's wife) and realized it's not that much different from a female locker room. Okay, clearly, the urinal things are different, but showers and toilets look the same.

And whether you are a male or female athlete, this is the place after every game, be it a win or a loss, where you go back to the same place of safety. It's not so much the room that is important as it is the people who occupy the space. What better way to celebrate a win than with the people who understand the sacrifice you made to bring home the victory, or, on the other hand, who better to swallow your pride with and accept that shameful loss.

As a player, guy or girl, I don't know if there's anyone better than those on the same team who you get to share life's ups and downs with, the team you practice with then go out and perform with. The improvements you all have seen each other make together makes being a team even more valuable. The tears you've cried and the aches and pains you've endured together made the weak team stronger.

Winning teams are built through tough times, and victories feel the best after you've suffered defeat. The locker room is the place to embrace either side of the coin toss. It's the place you regroup and rest during halftime. It's where friends are made, stories are shared and laughing occurs until your side hurts. Locker rooms were created with people in mind who will weather the storms of life with you. People who understand because they're in the exact same place as you. People who, like you, find shelter from a thunder storm when game delays stop progress and when tears cease to roll down your face after a championship loss or a defeated season.

Similarly, ladies, your home should be a safe place for your husband to go to and lay his head, laugh a little, and love a lot after a hard day's work. He should find comfort in knowing that safety can be found in the crevices of what he calls home. His secrets, career goals, and aspirations must be nailed to the walls of your heart and your prayers. You've got to assure him that he can confide in you and that he will receive confidence from your positive support, whether he wins or loses by the choices he makes in life. He's going to have to return back to the same place after every decision, whether the outcome is victory or defeat. Make sure it's a place where he can hold his head high despite the end result. He's counting on you, his team, to understand the "Ws" and the "Ls".

Wins and Losses

Prayer

Dear Jesus,

May we carry around in our bodies the remembrance of your death as we die daily to our fleshly desires and decisions so that your glory and your life will be revealed in us and through our marriages for others to witness. May we give grace when our husbands make mistakes, and when the world abandons them, may they find a home in our hearts.

In Jesus' name,
Amen!

Application & Transformation

Illumination: What are your thoughts concerning this devotional? What is God asking you to believe?

_____

_____

_____

_____

_____

Application: What is God asking you to **DO**?

_____

_____

_____

_____

_____

Transformation: The Holy Spirit has revealed His character to you through this study. **What is one thing you could change today that will make your character look more like His?**

_____

_____

_____

_____

_____

_____

28

Don't Look Back

"But Lot's wife, behind him, looked back, and she became a pillar of salt."

Genesis 19:26 ESV

If you're like me, you've had your share of packing boxes and hoping they all arrive at the correct front door on the expected delivery date. Most times, thank God, my family has received everything we placed on the moving truck, except this one time. After taking a couple of weeks to unpack everything from one of our moves, I noticed I had some of my favorite pairs of shoes missing. Then, some clothes, and then some more clothes and some more shoes. By now, I was searching frantically for the moving company's contact information. A girl couldn't let a good pair of shoes get lost in "Nowhere Land", right? I mean they were M.I.A. (missing in action) and I was issuing an A.P.B. (all-points bulletin) STAT!

The shoes and the clothes that were missing had more to do with what they represented than the price or the brand name associated with them. See, each pair of shoes was a stepping stone in our marriage and my career. Each article of clothing represented what stage of life we were in when I bought it and where that article of clothing was taking us. Like, that one nice business suit you wear to every interview 'cause it fits just right! Or those classic black heels that go with everything! Yeah, I couldn't let them go just yet!

When Ruth made the decision to follow Naomi, her mother-in-law, to Moab, she forsook everything she knew to experience something she hadn't known. The unfamiliar awaited her while the familiar screamed her return, but something inside of Ruth wouldn't allow her to turn back. She had no idea what was up ahead, but she knew there was nothing there for her to turn around and go back to. Her future was within her reach, if only she would keep moving **forward**.

After calling the moving company, the supervisor discovered that my entire wardrobe was still boxed up in our previous home's master bedroom closet. The movers had closed the door to the walk-in closet during the final walk-through and the boxes were still in there stacked like they'd left them. Many times we do the same. We close the door on our dreams, goals, and visions because we can't see past our current situations. We're too busy focusing on what we can see instead of believing God for what we can't. Truth is, I could have lived without those boxes of clothes and shoes. Hindsight reminded me that each outfit represented something in my past. I didn't necessarily need them. It just made me more comfortable to know that I had something familiar at my disposal. All of those clothes and shoes could have been replaced had they never been found.

If God has called you or your husband to a new job, new team, or new career, don't lose sight of your future holding on to your past. Take a look back, but never to return. Smile and reflect on how far you've come as you glance back at what was, but don't you dare use it to cancel out what shall be. Ignore your feelings and embrace your faith. You don't need what's familiar to succeed!

Don't Look Back

Prayer

⤳

Dear God,

Looking back is not the worst thing we could do in this world, but it is the worst place to remain. If we must look back on this coach's wife journey, may it be to remind us of how far we've come and how gracious you've been to us thus far. May we gaze our eyes instead on what's ahead because nothing in our rear view mirror will be needed for where you are taking us.

In Jesus' name,
Amen!

Application & Transformation

Illumination: What are your thoughts concerning this devotional? What is God asking you to believe?

_____

_____

_____

_____

_____

Application: What is God asking you to **DO**?

_____

_____

_____

_____

Transformation: The Holy Spirit has revealed His character to you through this study. ***What is one thing you could change today that will make your character look more like His?***

_____

_____

_____

_____

_____

29

Recruiting Rules

*"Have I not commanded you? Be strong and courageous. do
not be frightened, and do not be dismayed, for the Lord your
God is with you wherever you go."*
Joshua 1:9

I attended my very first American Football Coaches' Wives
Association Convention in 2017. It was in Nashville, Tennessee at
the Gaylord Opry Land Hotel. What a beautiful place to hang for
three whole days with my favorite coach!

After 13 years married, we were headed back to the place where
Hubs played his rookie year in the NFL with the Tennessee Titans.
So exciting! Not to mention, my best friend still lived there. I wish I
could tell Hubby the decision to accompany him was totally about

being with him, but I would have been lying. I sure couldn't wait to hug Nicole's neck again, either.

Getting to meet the other wives, the expectancy of what was to come, and getting to see John in his element was worth counting down the days. We arrived on a Sunday night to 25-degree weather and a very nice Uber driver. He dropped us off at Opry Land and it was everything I remembered it to be when we lived in "The 'Ville" (Nashville, that is). Swarms of men greeted us in the foyer. Hubs seemed to have known EVERYONE! I was patient with every *"What's up, Coach?"* and *"How you doin'?"* and every hug and handshake. It was like a big ole' family reunion for coaches.

Nevertheless, jet lag was settling in and it was past my bedtime. I took it on in as my coach chalked it up with some of his colleagues and compadres. The next morning I would say "hello" to "the better halves", but for now, after a long day of travel, I couldn't wait to close my eyes in restless anticipation.

Morning came and I was off to registration. Session One, entitled "How to Create a Financial Game Plan for Life," sparked my interest. I went in and found a seat. Then, after that session was over, I was off to Session Two, "Heels to Huddles". I had a feeling this session would be better than the first and everything about my assumption was right! As the day drew to a close, I remembered I was there at the convention with my husband and for him. I was ALL IN. We did separate things while we were there, but when evening hit, love always led us to the same place—our hotel room.

I was reminded on this trip that when my husband begins to recruit a high school player, he commits to that kid for sometimes two and maybe even three years, depending on the athlete's high school classification. The phone calls begin. The text messaging, the direct messaging, and then the home visits follow. It's like dating before popping the big question. In the end, after he's put the time and work in, my husband takes a risk at a 50/50 split. Either he will land a "no", or come out on top with a "yes". The ball is always in the recruit's court. Never the coach.

Life as it is affords us risks, also. The risk of moving your southern family to the west coast. The risk of opening up your mind to the new ideas at a coaches' wives convention. The risk of going back to the place that handed your husband a pink slip after his rookie year in the NFL and told him he wasn't good enough to remain on the team, yet he returns as a power five college coach, mentoring and teaching young men to play the same position he played.

The only rule to recruiting is staying committed. Find out all you need to know about this profession as a new wife. Spend time reading and learning the lingo. Get to know other wives who share similar stories. Attend some outings with your coach that are related to his career. Get on a plane in January and head to the annual convention with him. All of these things build your relationship. It's the glue that holds it all together.

Study your husband just as he studies film and the lives of those recruits. Why, you ask? Because author Jen Wilkins reminded me that "the heart cannot love what the mind does not know." Take time to go all in. There is a risk to becoming a better coach's wife, and it requires taking the time to "recruit" and win the heart for this game and the love of your husband.

Although risks may occur, you can be sure of this one thing: The Lord will determine how the dice fall. And based on his track record, if He doesn't get the one He goes after, they always come running back to Him! You got this, Sister!

Recruiting Rules

Prayer

Dear God,

I know there are risks that I must take to acquire the things that you have called me to in this season. Specifically, stepping out of my comfort zone to receive them. I place faith over fear, truth over doubt, and declare success over failure. May I be committed to your instructions and not frightened or dismayed when walking into unfamiliar territory. For you have already promised you are with me wherever I go. May I trust and believe that truth.

In Your matchless name, I pray,
Amen!

Application & Transformation

Illumination: What are your thoughts concerning this devotional? What is God asking you to believe?

_____

_____

_____

_____

_____

Application: What is God asking you to **DO**?

_____

_____

_____

_____

Transformation: The Holy Spirit has revealed His character to you through this study. ***What is one thing you could change today that will make your character look more like His?***

_____

_____

_____

_____

_____

30

Love Wins

We know how much God loves us, and we have put our trust in his love. God is love and all who live in love live in God, and God lives in them. And as we live in God our love grows more perfect.
1 John 5:16-17(a) (NLT)

As you prepare for a new season and the one you are currently in comes to a close, I implore you to put your trust in love. You may be asking, ***"What? Why? Put my trust in love? What does this have to do with sports?"*** And my response to you is this, "Yes, I thought it was a bit crazy too when God gave me these verses, but it's so much deeper than that." 1 John tells us that God is love. Therefore, put your trust in God because man may fail you, but love (God) never will.

As coaches' wives, most days we know this profession can be uncertain, but when we put our trust in God's love, not our husband's paycheck, not his job title, or the team that employs him, we learn to release all of our concerns and fears to God. On those days, when life throws us a curve ball or an incomplete pass, we can face them in love. Every set back and every disappointment is working God's revealed glory in us.

1 Corinthians chapter 13:7-8 teaches us love in this way:

*Love bears all things, believes all things, hopes all things, endures all things. Love **NEVER** fails.*

It would not be wise to put your trust in any ole' man, my friends. Instead, put your trust in The Man! As we profess to be God's children on this career path, we must "bear all things" in love. As God's child, you can rest assured that "all who live in love live in God and God lives in them" (1John 4:16). What a testimony as we transition through this life of sports to profess Christ not as much with what we say, but how we live and choose to love when adversity hits home. Will we choose to knock the ball out of the park, or just settle for stealing bases? Is Christ living in you by the way you show His love towards others and your husband? Are you leading others to Christ with your life? Do you bear fruit in love? If not, we've got some work to do, ladies. Want to be victorious over the enemy? LOVE in all circumstances. More reps and practice in this area will get you there. We lose when we don't love. Love has never lost a fight!

Love Wins

Prayer

Dear God,

May we find love even in the most challenging of times in our lives. May we find forgiveness and reconciliation on a daily basis as you so graciously give to us. May we, as coaches' wives, understand that if we don't win at home by loving, we lose in public while living. May our lives on the outside reflect our love for You and our husbands on the inside.

In Jesus' name,
Amen!

Application & Transformation

Illumination: What are your thoughts concerning this devotional? What is God asking you to believe?

_____
_____
_____
_____
_____

Application: What is God asking you to **DO**?

_____
_____
_____
_____
_____

Transformation: The Holy Spirit has revealed His character to you through this study. **What is one thing you could change today that will make your character look more like His?**

_____
_____
_____
_____
_____

31

Because You Fit

"Then the Lord God said, "It is not good that the man should be alone; I will make him a helper fit for him."
Genesis 2:18

This industry will throw you and your husband a lot of incomplete passes and perhaps some interceptions, but the two of you together will catch a host of touchdowns. Don't dwell on the strikes. Be grateful for home plate!

As his wife, it will be easy to sit and dwell on the mistakes, thinking how you went wrong, and how you failed, but don't fall for those feelings because God reminded you in Genesis that no matter what it looks like, you fit.

You fit as a coach's wife. You fit as a mom. You fit in the organization. You fit as a child of the Most High God. You fit in your husband's heart. You fit in the Kingdom of God.

Don't get distracted. Had you been too big or too little, the mold would have had to have been recreated, but it wasn't. The mold was created once for you and was never again duplicated. No one else was better for your husband. Believe it. Be brave in it, and walk in it.

You fit perfectly in the mold of what you two are created to do together. You fit perfectly in the grand scheme of God's plan for your lives. You fit as an assistant coach's wife and will fit as a head coach's wife if that is your husband's desire. Don't second guess it. You were created to "help" and "fit" the needs of your house and your husband and that looks differently in every home. So, do your husband a favor and walk in the fullness of your calling. Confidently. You were created from his side (Genesis 2:21) and made to stand by his side.

The ESV bible says a "**Helper** is one who supplies strength in an area that is lacking in the one who is helped."

"Fit for him" is defined as "matching him".

Dearest Coach's Wife,

Your role is so very important. Don't discount it. Don't allow anyone else to make you feel "less than" because of it. Supply the strength your husband needs in the areas where he is weak because you are the only woman who "fits" him. His rib is now your rib (Genesis 2:22). Protect what has been deposited into you at all costs. Cover him in prayer and count it ALL joy (James 1:2-3) in every season. Because we all know winning is sweeter when the entire team is there to witness it.

Because You Fit

Prayer

Dear Jesus,

When you created male and female, you made nothing else on earth like us. We were made for relationship with you. As a result, we get to be relational with others, especially the one we call husband. May we be his sounding board when the world around him is chaotic, and his strength when the weight of the world is on his shoulders. Thank you for "bringing me to my husband" (Genesis 2:23). It is the place I long to reside.
May I respect and honor this space, by his side, that You have created me to fit into.

In Jesus' name I pray,
Amen!

Application & Transformation

Illumination: What are your thoughts concerning this devotional? What is God asking you to believe?

_____

_____

_____

_____

_____

Application: What is God asking you to **DO**?

_____

_____

_____

_____

_____

Transformation: The Holy Spirit has revealed His character to you through this study. **What is one thing you could change today that will make your character look more like His?**

_____

_____

_____

_____

_____

Bonus

Find Your Voice

"...rather let it be the hidden person of the heart, with the incorruptible beauty of a gentle and quiet spirit, which is very precious in the sight of God."
1 Peter 3:3-4 (ESV)

I understand. You're trying to find your place beyond the field. You ask questions like, **When do I speak up? That jerk fired my husband! Should I speak up? I have all the right too! If I speak up do I run the risk of my husband, getting fired?**

My Answer: Hide your voice behind the Word of God.

What do I mean? Pray and seek God about EVERYTHING concerning your faith, your family, and football.

When you hide your voice behind His, you can't go wrong. Others may not agree with you, but the truth of the matter is, the Word of God doesn't lie. It is infallible (absolutely trustworthy). 2Timothy teaches us in 2:16, that "all scripture is given by inspiration of God, and is profitable for doctrine, for reproof, for correction, for instruction in righteousness, that the man of God may be complete, thoroughly equipped for every good work."

You have work to do, Sis. There's more to being his wife than being a trophy. What does that actually mean anyway? Oh, I know. My husband is a winner, and because I'm attached to him, I've attained the prize also! Not that I am *the* prize. Sister, you're more than a pretty face. You're more than a spicy, sassy, feisty, cheerleading sidekick. "Yes!"

You are a voice. A voice that matters. A voice that is important. A voice that should be heard, but in the right moment and at the proper time. Let respect and honor go before you. Allow prayer and grace to run ahead of you so that when you get to the place, the sound that echoes from you will come down from heaven. A gentle and quiet spirit, the bible says, is precious to God. And do you remember what Day 12's devotional taught us? In quietness and confidence shall be your strength. Sounds to me that God is not playing about a woman having a **quiet** spirit.

Settle yourself. If it burns that bad for you to speak up, you might not want to say anything. Words should come from a pure and forgiving heart, one full of grace and mercy, not from rage and anger. Talk to a trusted friend about what is bothering you, your pastor's wife, or a confidant that will pray you through this season in your life.

All words, pain, feelings of betrayal and hurt don't warrant a response. Some things are just better kept between you and God in the midst of prayer. Until you are free, silence your soul from the pain of what that person did to you or your husband. Continue in prayer for them and confess your sins to God. That is where the healing begins (James 5:16). Let your voice be one of prayer instead of a voice that points fingers.

You will not find your strength in quarreling. It will not only tear your house apart, but it will destroy the reputation and influence you and your husband are building.

Stay the course. God's got it all under control.

"Beloved, do not avenge yourselves, but rather give place to wrath; for it is written, "Vengeance is Mine, I will repay," says the Lord. (Romans 12:19)

Find Your Voice

Prayer

Dear God,

Thank you for the voice you have given me, but teach me how to use it in love. Help me to be patient and kind with it. Help me to edify and use it to build others up and not tear them down. And when silence is golden, remind me that keeping quiet is more valuable than all the riches in the world. The goal is to bring others to you with my words, not cause them to run away, and this includes my husband.

**In Jesus' name,
Amen!**

Application & Transformation

Illumination: What are your thoughts concerning this devotional? What is God asking you to believe?

_____

_____

_____

_____

_____

Application: What is God asking you to **DO**?

_____

_____

_____

_____

_____

Transformation: The Holy Spirit has revealed His character to you through this study. **What is one thing you could change today that will make your character look more like His?**

_____

_____

_____

_____

_____

Coaches' Wives Pray

I have asked some of my dearest coach's wife friends to add their special prayers, advice, and encouragement to this section of the devotional. All of these women are different and unique in their own right, yet one common goal brings us all together, and that is those sweet precious moments where we've all had to stop whatever we were doing and offer up our husbands to God in prayer.

Please take note. Recite these prayers over your husband if you can't find words of your own to say, and remember you have a team of women who have your back and are praying for, and pushing you forward along this faith journey that we get to experience with our favorite Coach's.

Two are better than one, because they have a good reward for their toil. For if they fall, one will lift up his fellow. But woe to him who is alone when he falls and has not another to lift him up!

Ecclesiastes 4:9-10

Dear Lord,

I know you have placed us in a special vocation. I am blessed with your protection and provision at all times through your unending love and favor. Please increase my patience so that I keep my eyes on you today. I will trust in you and your plans for all; they are so much better than mine.

Lord, transform me so that I will not conform to this world. Please help me to let the fruit of the Spirit flow through me and let me be a light to all that I know. When I am distracted by the devil, I will lean into you. I will have the life of love, joy and peace that you intend for our family and me. I praise you, Lord, for being a wonderful father.

In Jesus Christ Name,
AMEN!

"She is clothed with strength and dignity, and she laughs without fear of the future."
Proverbs 31:25

PENNI GRAHAM
FORMER FIRST LADY OF FOOTBALL
ARIZONA STATE UNIVERSITY

His Obedience

The coaching profession is a BIG business, that has created a culture of one always wanting to get to the "next level," whether it be a larger conference, more money, or always seeking a promotion. There's absolutely nothing wrong with aspiring to get to the "next level," but one must ensure that his/her aspirations are aligned with God's plan for his/her life. Oftentimes, I find myself praying that my husband continues to abide in Christ, walk in the power of the Holy Spirit, and remain obedient to God's will. That way, when a job/promotion is presented, he can clearly hear God's voice. God will guide him in making important decisions that will affect our lives. God will also help guide those day-to-day decisions and moment-by-moment decisions that also have a great impact.

Dear God,

Help my husband to be obedient to the guidance of the Holy Spirit. Help him to always trust and obey and to live a life that is holy. Please continue to reveal Yourself to him so that his steps can be ordered according to the plans You have set forth for his life.

Amen.

KIMBIA FOBBS
FIRST LADY OF FOOTBALL
GRAMBLING STATE UNIVERSITY

This is what I always tried to remember and live by:

- He's the players' coach, but he's my husband.

- I'm his number one fan and supporter.

- Whether he wins, loses or ties, there's another game to be played, the sun will come up in the morning, and God is always in control.

- And last, but certainly not least, I cast all my cares upon Him because He cares for me.

- This is my life's motto: "I don't worry"!

- It's just a game.

JULIET BALDWIN
FIRST LADY OF THE FIRST AFRICAN AMERICAN
COACH IN DIVISION 1 FOOTBALL

I pray that temptations are small, and that the Lord prepares you for my craziness and emotions. I pray He prepares you for leadership and me for submitting, that he softens your heart, grows your understanding of Him, opens your eyes more to see His grace, and prepares you for everything that might come. I pray you lean on Him and love Him more.

Amen.

CAROLYN GOLDING
WIFE OF PETE GOLDING / CO-DEFENSIVE COORDINATOR
ALABAMA CRIMSON TIDE

To our Coaches:

I would like to offer you encouragement to continue "walking in your purpose". God has not only called you to a profession, but to a platform. Everyday you have a fresh opportunity to pour into the lives of young men. You aren't coaching as an accident but as a witness and example to future generations of husbands, fathers, and leaders. Embrace it and ask the Lord to give you wisdom, strength, and consistency when you feel a lack of control over your future.

"Trust in the Lord with all your heart and lean not on your own understanding; In all your ways acknowledge Him, And He shall direct your paths."
Proverbs 3:5-6

ROMONDA JORDAN,
WIFE OF RANDY JORDAN
RUNNING BACK COACH WASHINGTON REDSKINS

Father God,

Thank you for my husband. I lift him up to you, Lord. He is yours before he is mine. I speak life and hope in those places I could never see, feel or know. You know his needs far more than what I can comprehend. You know his frustrations, his temptations and the limitations he puts on himself and even on You. I pray You forgive his unbelief and strengthen his faith. I pray he releases everything unto you that weighs him down. Your word says that your yoke is easy and your burden is light. I pray he chooses to live light so that his career

will not become a burden but will always remain a blessing. I pray he recognizes that his position is for divine leadership first and that anything else comes second. I pray he won't be moved by losses but maintain an attitude of victory in his spirit. When time gets difficult, I pray you refresh him with your promise, and light under him the passion to work diligently on his job as if he was working unto You. Forgive him for ever putting his career before you. Forgive him for choosing plays, film or practice over you. Help him prioritize his time in the order of importance and forgive him for ever making basketball an idol in his life. Give him a healthy love for the game so it will never take Your position in his heart. Give him vision for his career. Help him understand what it is You would like for him to accomplish in coaching, not what he wants, and then let him pursue that with all his heart, no matter the cost. Thank you for choosing my husband to be the light in the dark world of sports. And as he continues to go forth in his career, please Lord, keep his fire burning for You.

In Jesus' name,
Amen.

ERICKA ELLIS
WIFE OF TYRONE ELLIS
PHOENIX SUNS ASSISTANT COACH

Conclusion

My desire for this coaches' wives devotional was never to point fingers at who does what in their marriage and who doesn't. That's certainly not my business. The finger I am pointing is in an upward position, and that is to remind all of us that our marriages should look like Christ. When my husband and I sat down at our kitchen table to brain storm thoughts for this devotional, our desire was for every coaches' wife and coach who picked this devotional up to take a look inside themselves and say, "What can I do better to improve my marriage?" Not, "What can my husband or wife do better."

I have learned over 15 years of marriage and 19 years of dating my husband that it is not John's responsibility to make me happy. It's my responsibly to allow our marriage to make me holy.

I pray this devotional has done the same for you. Your marriage has been designed to give God glory and to show all the world what it looks like for Jesus to come back for His bride in the sports entertainment industry. I am praying your marriage exceeds the test of time. You two are a team. Play to WIN!

Blessings from our team to yours!

Cecelia Simon

is a writer, speaker, and wife of retired NFL pro athlete, John Simon. She is the founder of Caterpillar's Transformed, a ministry she has been given the platform to help young and seasoned women "transform lives into the beauty of creation" according to Romans 12:2. In addition to her duties in ministry, Cecelia is a student at Phoenix Seminary where she is currently pursuing a second Master's degree in Biblical and Theological Studies.

After graduating from high school with honors, Cecelia attended Louisiana Tech University where she obtained her undergraduate degree in Business Administration and went on to complete her first Masters of Arts in Counseling degree from Dallas Baptist University along with an Advanced Certification in School Counseling. She taught middle school, Language Arts and Reading, for a number of years and then became an elementary school Guidance Counselor for the remainder of her years as an Educator.

When Cecelia is not pursuing her career endeavors she enjoys shopping, cheering for her husband's team, and spending time with their two sons. They currently reside in Phoenix, Arizona where her husband is the running backs coach and assistant head coach at Arizona State University.

Cecelia Simon

To book Cecelia for your next book club, workshop, or speaking event go to:

www.CeceliaSimon.com

OR email: caterpillarstransformed@gmail.com

Please join Cecelia and a community of other coaches' wives on **Instagram @CoachesWivesUnite** as she inspires other coaches' wives to:

- LEARN - marriage through biblical principles
- LOVE - our coaches unconditionally &
- LIVE - our best lives wherever this sport takes us

OTHER RESOURCES FROM
Cecelia

AVAILABLE NOW!

This book is for those who have lost hope along this journey called life. Somewhere between the start and finish line you gave up, threw in the towel…quit! As a result, your dreams were shattered and you've settled for less than what God has for you.

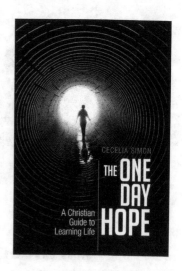

Well, the good news is, the choices you make today will determine what happens to your tomorrow. You don't have to have it all together. You don't have to know what your purpose is in life. Hope is free, but it takes courage, faith, and perseverance from your inner most being to get to where God has created you to be.

I challenge you after reading this book to forget about your past and walk into your future. Hope is here for you now!

www.ceceliasimon.com